UNLOCKING YOUR CREATIVITY

Inspired: Unlocking Your Creativity

published by Kidmin Academy

edited by Tina Houser

copyright ©2018

cover design by Vanessa Mendozzi

CONTENTS

INTRODUCTION

FIRST OF ALL ... THANKS for picking up this book. It has been a real treat to put together. I am convinced that you're going to enjoy reading it and that you're going to find it beneficial for doing children's ministry. Ministry to children provides a plethora of ways to use your creativity and to encourage your team to do likewise. Having an outlet for your ideas is one of the things that makes kidmin so endearing and so downright fun. Other adults look forward to putting on a costume one day a year, but kidmin can do it whenever they please. Other adults sit quietly in their cubicles, but kidmin get to yell a high-energy countdown into a megaphone. Other adults have a meltdown when they get a ketchup spot on their shirt from a misplaced fry at lunch, but kidmin live to have slime poured over their heads. This ministry God has called you to is crazy and creative!

When my family goes through my things when I die, they're going to find ideas jotted on scraps of paper, napkins that have scribbles on them, computer files under a host of labels, notes and handouts from conferences, and baskets filled with index cards. They represent so many ideas that have made my eyes light up, but there just wasn't enough time to put them all into action. Each one describes a creative way I've thought of myself or a way that a fellow kidmin has used to reach kids for the Kingdom of God. Without a doubt, you can minister to children without using much creativity, but it's like adding some hot sauce to a dish when you spice up your program or event with your own unique ideas.

I love the feeling of fresh, of new, of doing something for the first time. Why? Because it usually means my creativity has been active. The switch is flipped to "ON!" I'm convinced that a lot of churches decide to change curriculum not because it no longer meets the needs of their kids, but because the teachers have taught it before and they need the new activities a different curriculum brings. A different curriculum activates their creativity. The curriculum I personally wrote for KidzMatter is on a 3-year scope and sequence, and I teach with it almost every week. The fourth year is always a difficult one for me, because I remember teaching those same lessons three years earlier. I'm familiar with it, and one of the things that makes me feel creative is to present a fresh activity to the kids. The thing I forget, though, is that it IS fresh to those kids, because they've never experienced it, but it's not fresh to me because I remember how it went with the last group of kids. That's one of the reasons it's so important to give your team members permission to insert their creativity into the lessons they teach or the time they spend with kids.

In the pages that follow, you're going to be challenged to stretch your creativity to new levels. You're going to be encouraged if for some reason you think God left the creative bone out of your body. You're going to gain knowledge about how creativity actually works. You're going to gather ideas that may open a whole new area of ministry possibilities for you. And, you're going to be inspired to use your creativity to glorify the Creator God.

A host of amazing kidmin have contributed to the content. What they bring to you in each chapter represents the successes and failures they've had along the way. They share the lessons they've learned about how to lasso creativity and direct it to make the biggest impact in this world for Jesus. So, get out your highlighter and enjoy your exploration of the amazing attribute God placed in you—creativity.

In His incredible joy,

Tina Houser

chapter 1

WHAT'S GOING ON IN YOUR BRAIN?

*Networks, daydreaming, hydration,
and taking out the trash*

BY TINA HOUSER

ONE OF THE MOST BASIC PIECES of information you've been taught about your brain is that the left side is where all the logical thinking takes place, while the right brain is where your creativity happens. Not so! Erase that false information right now ... unlearn it. That information is far too simple for a very complex organ. Very recent research indicates we've been operating under false understandings. It seems like each day, the exploration of the brain "blows your mind" in a whole new way!

So, what is true? In the next few pages, I want to explore what's going on in the brain that helps you tap into creativity. I'm regularly flabbergasted by the complexity of the three pounds of grey matter that's housed in a person's skull. Some people are fascinated by discovering healthy foods and fitting them into their lifestyle. Others spend decades anticipating the exotic lands they'll experience in retirement. Someone else loves the smell of raw wood and carves out every extra moment to be in their woodworking shop. Me? Well, I absolutely love learning one more tidbit about how God, in His off-the-charts creativity, assembled the human brain. It always leaves me in a stunned state of amazement.

The research that has been conducted in the last few years (published in the *Proceedings of the National Academy of Sciences*) indicates that, contrary to popular belief, creativity is not housed in a particular part of the brain. In stark contrast, it actually takes place throughout the brain. The entire brain gets in on the process of creativity. It seems like no one wants to be left out of the fun party of creating! The reason for this is that creativity is encouraged when regions of the brain that don't usually work together engage with one another. Read that again: regions of the brain that don't usually work together engage with one another. Doesn't that make a lot of sense? The actual meaning of creativity is connecting ideas and objects that don't usually work together, in order to do something brand new. You think of creativity as coming up with a use for something that is totally out of the ordinary—something you had previously never connected it with. You make sense of something that's never had a connection before.

That requires a lot of brain flexibility! (Okay, I just had a funny mental picture—a brain bending, stretching, doing yoga. Sorry, just had to share how my entire brain is wandering around this topic.)

THREE NETWORKS

Instead of looking at left-brain and right-brain, scientists have identified three networks in the brain. One network is called the "default" network, because when nothing else is going on, when you're not concentrating on something, this is where your thoughts go. Daydreaming and mind-wandering happen in the default network, as well as brainstorming (where you clear the mechanism and have an undisturbed flow of thoughts). We know that daydreaming, mind-wandering, and brainstorming all support the process of creativity, so it's not far-fetched to associate the default network of the brain with the creative process.

The second network is known as the "executive control" network. Think of an executive of a company who needs to keep employees focused and on task. He's the manager of what's taking place. What's taking place in the executive control brain network is the working memory (storing information and being able to access it) and being able to articulate that stored information. This is the network that focuses and keeps the brain on task, and then is able to tell you what it's been up to.

The third network of the brain that's vital to creativity is the "salience" network. "Salience" means important and particularly noticeable. This network decides what thoughts need your attention. It decides how you're going to react to what's going on and what you're thinking. It determines your perception and may pull in an emotional response to the thought or idea. The salience network puts a spotlight on the thought and brings it to the forefront ... ding, ding, ding ... it alerts you to "this is a good possibility!"

As you can see, the functions of each of these networks are not ones that normally work together. But, the ability to get them to talk to one another enhances creativity. Your brain puts together functions that you don't think of as going together ... just like a new idea comes from putting two things together that you don't usually think of as going together (like using Styrofoam cups to teach the books of the Bible—those two aren't usually associated with one another). Ta-da ... creativity!

Let's take a look, in the simplest form, how the research was conducted. Everything was done while the participants were undergoing an MRI to watch their brain activity. I doubt if your budget allocates for an MRI machine. You can't do the MRI part, but just for the fun of it, you may want to conduct the non-MRI exercise with your team. Participants were shown an object, like a brick. In 30 seconds, they had to identify as many uses for the object as possible. The responses were ranked according to how many participants gave the same answer. If a large number of the participants gave the same answer, the individual points awarded would be low. If it was a unique answer given by only one participant, then the points awarded would be high. The MRI showed that brain activity across the three networks was high in those people who scored high (having original ideas). The three networks which don't normally converse with one were firing information back and forth. These networks were busy working with one another and the creative output was high.

The ease with which a person's brain moves from one network to another is a strong indicator of how creative they are. Their brains are able to coordinate the three networks, which takes a great deal of brain flexibility. So, even without asking the participant to do anything, you can assume that if the MRI shows activity within all three networks at the same time, then this is someone you would consider creative.

DAYDREAMING

As a forerunner to the recent findings about the three networks, for decades, psychologists have studied daydreaming. Recall that daydreaming is part of the default network. The researchers concluded long before they understood how all three networks work together, that daydreaming is important to creativity. Rather than being self-standing as they previously thought, daydreaming works with the other two networks to strengthen creativity.

When charged with the responsibility to come up with a creative solution to a problem, more than likely your approach is to focus on it until a solution surfaces. You keep your head down and push forward. "I'm not leaving until I solve this!" is the attitude that washes over you. But, according to a team of researchers at the University of California at Santa Barbara, that's not the most beneficial way to produce a satisfactory result. They found that the research participants who were given a break to let their minds wander came back to the problem with more creative solutions than those participants who were not given daydreaming time.

What can you take away from the daydreaming research? A couple of things. When you get bogged down in trying to figure out a problem—how to handle parents picking up their kids at the end of VBS, or how to you stabilize a 25-foot ship mast in the sanctuary, or the best way to advertise an upcoming family event—walk away. Go to your "happy place." (Mine is envisioning myself on the island of Kauai.) Daydream. The other take-away is to treat yourself each day with a little time to let your mind wander ... even if there's not a problem that needs solving. This little daily blessing will strengthen the network connections in your brain. Bet you didn't realize that daydreaming was exercise for your creative "muscles." Consequently, you're strengthening your ability to be creative.

HYDRATION AND SLEEP

Your brain is 75% water. When that 75% of your brain has its full amount of water, the result is better focus, faster mental processing, and ... you guessed it ... more creativity! When you sit down to think creatively and find yourself with droopy eyelids, it very well may be that you need a bottle of water. Don't fool yourself, though, into thinking that a cup of coffee or a can of pop will perk you up. They actually do the exact opposite and dehydrate you. Although you think the caffeine will wake up your brain, what your brain really needs and is crying out for is water. Coffee and pop become the "trash" that we're going to talk about in a moment.

How can a good night's sleep impact your creativity? Ah, the brain is at it, again! The University of Rochester Medical Center for Translational Neuromedicine released a study showing that slumber gives your brain a chance to clear out potentially harmful waste that builds up while you're awake.

So, here's what happens. While you're asleep, your brain "takes out the trash." Imagine a little garbage truck going through your brain each night to collect everything that shouldn't be there—all the toxins and overstock of nutrients. If you cut back on the number of hours you sleep, the garbage truck may not have enough time to make its rounds. The process of taking out the brain trash is called the glymphatic system and it's ten times more active when you're sleeping than when you're awake.

This is what happens during this glymphatic process. The waste within the cells is actually flushed out of your brain cells by pumping cerebral spinal fluid through them. The flushing removes the waste (trash). A crazy thing happens when you sleep. Your brain cells shrink by 60%! The shrinkage allows for the cerebral spinal fluid to flow faster and more freely. Think flash flood that washes away everything in its path. Pumping all that fluid, though, takes a lot of energy—energy that doesn't seem to be available when you're awake and engaging actively in everything that goes on during your day. If the energy is only available when you sleep, and the brain cells desperately need to have their waste removed, then it's imperative that you realize the importance of a good night's sleep.

Doesn't it also make sense, then, that when your brain is healthy (hydrated and free of garbage) that the three networks we discussed earlier would function better ... thus increasing your ability to be creative?

It absolutely makes my head feel like it's going to explode when I try to take in all God did in designing the human brain ... and that was just one little part of His vast creation. He is the ultimate Biologist, Geneticist, and Neurologist! *God made the human brain ... and He said, "It is good!"*

Tina Houser loves all things kidmin. She's a wife of 42 years, mother, children's pastor, author of 18 books, speaker, coach, and editor (of this book and many others). Her favorite title, though, is to be lovingly called Silly Grandma by her 3 grand-kiddos (plus all the kids at church and on the ballfield who have now followed suit). Tinahouser.net

chapter 2

PAINTING, PLANNING, AND PRAYING

How to learn creativity

BY JULIA BALL

I HAVE TO MAKE A CONFESSION right from the start of this chapter: I am horrible at arts and crafts. If you think I'm exaggerating, just ask my 5th-grade art teacher. I still remember coming home with a 70 on my report card in art and being devastated!

Art was supposed to be an easy subject! It was supposed to be fun! I wasn't supposed to get a 70. From 5th grade moving forward, I had a tumultuous relationship with art. I vividly remember having to stay after school (the only time ever!) the next year to complete a basket weaving project that everyone else had done during class time.

I kept that basket for years as a reminder of how long it took me to complete a simple art project. I always avoided art electives in high school; instead, I opted for classes like writing and theatre arts. In university, my arts credits were in music and English. I avoided like the plague anything that had to do with paintbrushes or colored markers!

You can imagine then, how ironic it felt when I became a full-time children's pastor. So much of children's ministry is rooted in creativity, whether it's making VBS props, designing a set, or coming up with an art project or craft. While some people may find themselves overwhelmed with volunteer recruiting or organizational structures in children's ministry, I'm not that person. Give me a spreadsheet, an email list, and a theological concept to break down and I'm good to go. But, if you put a craft in front of me and ask me to make a sample ... well, I automatically break into a cold sweat.

Despite my (somewhat irrational) fear of art and craft projects, I've found, over time, that being creative in children's ministry is something I really enjoy. While it may not come naturally to me, I've learned, and am still learning, how to be creative.

One of the first things I had to determine when I started in children's ministry is that I had to stop telling myself I wasn't creative. I discovered quickly that while I may not be good at the stereotypically creative things, there were other areas where I could use creativity and thrive. While most people may not think of creativity and organization in the same sentence, I realized that the way I could imagine a spreadsheet or schedule and put it into action was in itself, a form of being creative.

The fact that I love music (even if I'm not good at the actions) helped me recognize that creativity takes diverse forms. Recognizing a good worship song takes just as much creative energy as pumping out an incredible craft.

You see, I put limits on my own creativity without even realizing it. Because I had painted a picture in my mind of what creative people did, or what they were gifted at, I sold myself short. As I began to perceive areas where my creative juices were already flowing, I started to build more confidence to experiment with creativity in other areas of ministry.

Once I embarked on the work of stopping that negative thought train, I had to start the equally hard work of working at being creative. Initially, this seemed like an oxymoron to me. I thought creativity was supposed to come naturally! Was I really being creative if I forced myself to try? Wasn't that faking it?

Well, maybe it was faking it, but it actually did help. Regularly, I set aside time in my office just for the sake of being creative. Pinterest was a huge help in the initial stages. (Okay, who am I kidding, it still is!) I explored simple craft projects, decorating ideas, and bulletin board set-ups and tried them.

I still remember one of the first bulletin board displays I attempted. As I opened that crisp package of paper and pictures from Oriental Trading, I felt confident. I quickly became dismayed, though, when there were no instructions inside the packaging—just a picture of what it could look like at the end. I wanted instructions! I needed direction! I needed help to achieve this creative goal!

Well, creating that bulletin board display took way longer than it should have. It looked nothing like the package. I was slightly disappointed. But yet, I felt proud. I had done something somewhat creative. I was learning! And despite it being stressful, I actually kind of enjoyed it!

That first bulletin board display was the start of a host of creative activity in my ministry. Regularly changing up those displays, switching up the layout and decorations in classrooms, and making little gifts for kids or volunteers became a more regular part of my work routine. They took a long time for me to accomplish, way longer than a spreadsheet or schedule, but I found myself fulfilled.

After a while, a funny thing started to happen. People around me started to comment on how creative I was!

INSPIRED: UNLOCKING YOUR CREATIVITY

Honestly, I felt like laughing. Me? Creative? This was the girl who got 70% in 5th-grade art, remember? I wasn't creative! I was just working hard!

With time though, I realized that creativity may come naturally to some people, but for others of us, it's learned. It takes discipline, planning, and practice. As I disciplined myself to be creative, I discovered that I could actually do some pretty creative things.

I also learned that creativity isn't limited to arts and crafts in children's ministry. Creativity comes in the way you teach children the Bible. It can even come in the way you structure a schedule or plan volunteer meetings. It comes in the way you do outreach, and the methods you choose to disciple. Creativity must infiltrate every part of your ministry, not just the obvious parts.

It took me thinking I wasn't creative to actually learn how to be. It took me disciplining myself to spend time doing creative activities to start thinking creatively all the time, not just in those few moments.

I'm still not a creative genius, but I've learned a few lessons along the way. So if you're feeling a little uncreative in your ministry, here are some of my best tips.

1. PRACTICE BEING CREATIVE!

Set aside some time to practice creativity, both at home and at work. Since deciding I would be more intentionally creative, I've attempted all sorts of projects both for my home and my ministry—whether something as simple as the bulletin board display I described or something as complex as trying to make seasonal pillowcases for my couch. (Full disclosure: they did not look like the Pinterest picture.) I've worked at integrating creativity into my everyday life.

My challenge to you then, if you want to learn how to be creative, is to take some time to actually do it! Grab a paintbrush, some markers, or a needle and thread. Take to Pinterest and browse through the DIY section until you find something that seems relatively simple and go for it!

2. PLAN TO BE CREATIVE.

It's so easy in children's ministry to get stuck in the rut of doing the same thing over and over. If your curriculum doesn't make space for you to be creative in planning or activities, start creating that space anyway.

I try to schedule into my calendar regular events or lessons that force me to invent and create. I challenge myself to teach on a topic that I can't find a curriculum on, so I'm forced to invent and create something. I find a super cool art project online, and decide I'm going to teach it to the kids, even if all of theirs turn out better than mine! I'll never learn how to be more creative if I don't plan for it. This may sound very uncreative, but it actually works.

3. PRAY ABOUT CREATIVITY.

One of the greatest things I've learned about being creative is that our God is the ultimate Creator. The Holy Spirit is the most creative being on the planet. We simply need to take a glance at the world we live in and the people we cross paths with to see that our God is a creative God.

When I intentionally pray and ask God to give me creative ideas—not just for art projects, but for outreach, discipling, and connecting with parents—I've been blown away at the light bulb moments I've had. Various ministry events, lesson plans, and even organizational structures have been born that I could never have come up with on my own. As you partner with God, ask Him not just for wisdom and strength in ministry, but creativity. He will come alongside you and breathe ideas into you that you could never have created on your own.

4. HAVE A CREATIVITY FILE.

This idea actually came into being after hearing Fredrik Haren speak at the Global Leadership Summit in 2017. His talk was all about ideas and how important it is as leaders to be constantly dreaming up new ideas, regardless of your field of work!

Haren has actually produced *The Idea Book*, which is a unique journal designed just to come up with ideas! (Check out FredrikHaren.com for details.) While I didn't buy the book at the conference (children's pastor budget, am I right?), I did come home and start regularly writing down ideas I had. Even if they weren't good ones, I stowed them away in a journal or in the notes section on my iPhone. Anytime I get an idea related to ministry, whether while in the office or walking down an aisle at Walmart, I try to jot it down.

Most of the ideas are no-go's. When I look back on them, they're not that great. Every now and then, however, I come across one and think, "Wow! That was such a good idea! I can't believe I thought of that!" If I didn't take the time to jot down those thoughts, I would never have come up with some of the greatest ministry ideas and plans I've had so far. When I'm feeling particularly uninspired, I flick through those notes to remind myself, "I may not have a good idea today, but I've had lots in the past, and I will again sometime!"

So I encourage you, open up your own creativity file! Whether on your iPhone, computer, Pinterest board, or in a good old-fashioned notebook, find a space to write down those ideas and do it often. You never know when the next great inspiration may strike!

5. DO EVERYDAY TASKS CREATIVELY.

This is one of the practices I've implemented that has helped me the most. Each day, I try to do at least one regular task a little bit differently. At first, it was very deliberate; now it almost comes naturally!

Let me give you an example. I'm a note-taker. I take notes on everything: sermons, talks, videos, and meetings. A while ago, I became fascinated with the idea of calligraphy and fancy lettering. I haven't done any training or classes, but I wanted to try to record my notes creatively. I experimented with different styles of handwriting, designs on the page, and lettering ideas. While I always doodled, this is a little more intentional creativity. As I do this, I just naturally feel more creative! I'm accomplishing something, and I'm creating something that is (somewhat) beautiful.

Sometimes, it's other tasks—whether organizing a cupboard, sorting a drawer, or putting books on a shelf—that I'll try to do creatively. I ask myself, "How can I make this look nice?" "How can I use my imagination?" "Is there a better way to do this?" It may take a little extra time or effort, but I feel like I'm actually accomplishing something!

What everyday tasks can you start doing creatively? Maybe it's as simple as blasting some music and dancing around your office or kitchen as you go through your everyday routine. Maybe it's using colorful paper and nice fonts on your next spreadsheet or schedule to make it look nice! Or maybe it's color coding your books in your office to add a sense of beauty. Whatever it is, let me challenge you to take up an everyday task and do it with some pizazz!

Back to my 5th-grade art class. Part of my struggle in art was I tried too hard. I wanted everything to be perfect and look perfect. I often didn't get projects done because I spent way too much time on one little line or picture. I wanted step-by-step instructions and didn't really use my imagination or let myself be creative.

Creativity is a skill I've had to learn. As I've learned it, my ministry has been better because of it. I've learned to love creativity, and put it into practice in my everyday life. I believe that you can do that too, whether you're a 5th-grade art dropout like me or a modern-day Picasso! God has gifted each of you uniquely for His kingdom, and when you partner your creative juices with His, you can be unstoppable!

Julia Ball is a proud mom of a rambunctious 1-year-old and wife to super pastor and dad, Andrew. She currently serves as Children's and Family Pastor in Clarenville, Newfoundland, Canada, and Provincial Children's Director for her denomination. You can find her online at ministrymom.ca.

chapter 3

BAKE THE PERFECT DESSERT

Explore the creative process

BY LUCINDA GIBSON

I OFTEN GET ASKED where I get my creative and, most of the time crazy, ideas for lessons, activities, and events for our children's ministry. My standard answer is: "They usually come to me in the shower." This statement holds some truth. Many ideas are sparked when I'm involved in a routine activity such as a shower, laundry, or cooking supper. The truth of the matter is those ideas didn't just come to me in the shower and presto the event occurred. A whole process was followed to get myself from light bulb moment to completed activity with my kids. It's like creating the perfect dessert to celebrate a special occasion. You don't just decide to create a spectacular dessert, snap your fingers, and have a Pinterest worthy masterpiece. You follow a process from idea to masterpiece. It's a process that many do not see. Some will never know the time and effort put into the process. They only see the final product, yet it is the process that gets you to the product.

THE DECISION TO CREATE

First you start with the decision to create. Say you have a reason to celebrate, maybe a birthday, and you decide the best way to celebrate is to make the most amazing cake your loved one has ever seen. You have made the decision to create.

In ministry your decisions to create may be driven by your calendar, your vision and goals, or your convictions that your kids need to be taught a certain concept of God or Bible skill. Some decisions to create are simply driven by your calendar. Every year you're going to celebrate holidays, some in bigger ways than others. For instance, I know every year I'm going to take the four Wednesdays between Thanksgiving and Christmas to teach a unit on Christmas ending with a Christmas party. I need to create. Recently, our church had a prayer summit and it was decided that the format would be long and boring for kids. I suggested I lead a special kids' prayer summit. I needed to create. Some decisions are driven by your vision, goals, or large church emphasis.

If you're leading without a purpose in mind, are you just leading your people to wander around aimlessly? If you have goals and a vision but you aren't creating to that purpose, why do you have them? This year our church staff decided to lead our church in a year-long emphasis to be People of the Word with a reading plan. The decision to create was made for me in that I needed to create a way for the kids of our church to be involved in a manner that would have kingdom impact on their lives. Thus, the sword challenge was born.

Some decisions to create are led by a conviction of something your kids really need to learn about God or a Bible skill you see lacking in your group. Earlier this year I felt a great need for some lessons on seeing truth about ourselves in the way God sees us. The conviction led me to create our summer theme: Incredible Me, Seeing Myself the Way God Sees Me.

The decision to create is sometimes driven by inspiration from other children's ministry leaders. Seeing what others in children's ministry are doing often sparks inspiration to create. My own inspiration is sparked at trainings and conferences, getting together with others involved in children's ministry, and certainly not least by Facebook. I have several friends on Facebook who are involved in ministry and regularly post activities from their church. Facebook groups specifically designed for children's ministers are a wealth of inspiration for ideas. Creation is not going to happen without the decision to create.

GATHERING IDEAS

The decision to create has been made. Now the time has come to decide how you are going to create. You've decided you want to make your loved one a fabulous dessert but what kind of dessert are you going to make? You scour the internet, googling, searching Pinterest for the perfect dessert. You pin ideas and jot down notes on a notepad. You pull out all of your favorite cookbooks and cooking magazines and mark pages with Post-It notes. You look for the perfect dessert.

The same is true for creating in ministry. This part of the process varies in length for me. For those events that are driven by the calendar or that I know I need to create well in advance, this part of the process can be many months or even year-round. As I am writing this I have just wrapped up our VBS. Towards the end of the week, we released next year's theme. My mind instantly went to the gather ideas part of the process. In the two weeks before VBS my mind raced with ideas for fall and our Christmas theme. It can be overwhelming, but my mind is always busy with ideas for upcoming events and lessons. Therefore, a little organization is needed during this part of the process. A place to keep all these ideas is essential and you have to work the system that works for you.

One of the places I gather inspiration is Pinterest. Once I decide to create, one of the first things I do is designate a Pinterest board. In preparation for this summer I created a summer 2018 board and pinned anything and everything that looked interesting. I also create a notebook in my Evernote app. Evernote is a note-taking app that allows you to group notes into notebooks and save items from the web. As I move along in the process I often change the names of my notebooks. I began months ago with a notebook called Summer. I jotted down ideas. When I decided I wanted the focus be on God-esteem, I put that at the top of my idea page. Anytime I had an idea I jotted it down on that page. When the idea came to me, (actually in the shower), to use the minions from *Despicable Me,* I jotted that down in my notes and started pinning minion crafts. Maybe you're more of a pen and paper type person. Have a place in your notebook where you can put your ideas, use Post-It notes, or put pages in your planner for upcoming events. Keep a file folder where you collect ideas or a bulletin board. Just make sure you have a place to collect ideas and know where those ideas are when you move on to the next part of the process.

During this part of the process you may be looking for themes or broad event ideas. You may be looking for a starting place. Start with that decision to create. What is driving you to create? Consider what is popular with the kids at this moment. What is relatable to the kids? What holidays are near the event? What season of the year is this taking place? A few years back I wanted to take some time and focus on Bible skills. I looked at doing this focus during March and our annual March Madness was born complete with brackets and basketball fun.

An important detail of this part of the process is to take note of anything that might be useful. Will you use every idea? No. Just like in deciding to bake a dessert, you would not use every idea and recipe you liked. This part is just a brainstorming and gathering portion of the process.

FINALIZE YOUR RECIPE

At some point you have to move on to the next part of the process. If all you ever do is gather ideas, your dessert is never going to get baked. You have to take time to go back through the recipes you saved and decide what you're going to make. Maybe you're going to take a cake recipe from one place and pair it with icing from another and decorations from a third. Make your plan. Eliminate ideas that are not a good fit. You have to think about your loved one and what they love. What will make them happy?

The same is true in planning for your ministry. This is the point when you nail down a plan. The first step in this part of the process is prayer. I'm not saying you should not pray earlier in the process, but I believe prayer is vital at this time. You want God to guide you in your planning. If you're being creative and having fun but not in line with where God wants to be, your creativity is useless. You pray throughout the whole process, but you spend concerted time in prayer during this part.

This focused prayer will help you answer the questions that will narrow down your recipe for success. What is your purpose? Does this activity, theme, or idea add to fulfilling your purpose? It may be bushels of fun, but if it doesn't contribute to your end goal, do you really need to spend your energy on it. Who is your audience? Get to know your kids. How do they learn? What activities do they respond to best? If you're planning something for your entire ministry, make sure your kids are experiencing learning in a variety of ways. Not all kids learn the same. My Sunday school teachers have noted how each of our groups have different personalities as a group. Each year as the groups move through they have to teach differently. What do your kids respond to? How much time do you have for this lesson or event? How much time do you have to prepare for this event? Will this activity be possible in the space you are working? Be realistic with yourself. Be honest.

By answering these questions you can formulate your plan. If it's a lesson, do you have a format you follow each week? Outline your format and fill in your activities and your plan. If you're planning a unit or series of lessons, outline your weeks and what you wish to focus on each week. If you're planning a large event, outline your time. Fill in actions that need to be at certain times, such as food. Start with what you know are absolute musts and fill in the rest.

This is where your collected notes and pins on Pinterest come in to play. Scour through your ideas. Trash ideas that you know won't work. Mark them off. Delete them. Place ideas into your plans. You very likely will have way more ideas than are reasonable to put into place. Prayerfully choose the best. Which ideas will convey your message to the kids in an impactful way? Which ideas are the most reasonable to follow through and complete? If you get frustrated take a break. Walk away from the plan.

Come back to it on a later day. Spend some time in personal worship and communion with God. Sometimes you need to let the ideas marinate. Sometimes you need to remove yourself completely and enjoy time with God, enjoy time with your family, or just rest. When you return to the planning you return with fresh perspective, and it's more likely that everything will fall into place. When this portion of the process is complete, you have a plan. You're finished with the recipe.

ASSEMBLE THE INGREDIENTS AND BAKE THE CAKE

Planning is great. It gives you direction. If you stop after the plan, though, you have accomplished nothing except for wasting your time. You've decided on the perfect recipe to wow your loved one and make them feel special. If you set the recipe up and never head to the grocery store for the ingredients or actually make the cake, your loved one will never know how very special you think they are.

Ministry is the same. You can plan all day. You can come up with scads of great ideas, but if you never carry them out, you have just wasted your time. This is the part of the process where you put the rubber to the road and make things happen. Go through your plan and make a To-Do list. Add these items to your upcoming plans to make sure they get done.

- Is this an event that needs marketing? Add it to your To-Do list.

- Do you need to communicate any items with other staff members?

- Do you need to communicate with volunteers?

Once you've made your To-Do list, start marking things off the list. Put your plan into action and prepare for your lesson, activity, or event. Mix the ingredients, bake the cake, and decorate.

SAVOR EVERY BITE AND REMEMBER

Your cake is baked. The decorations are perfect. You present it to your loved one. They are overwhelmed by your gesture. You cut the cake and enjoy every bite. The end of the creative process is the culmination of your hard work. Lead your lesson or activity. Conduct your event. Enjoy the moments with your kids. When it is all over take a moment to thank God for what He has done, ways He worked, and lessons He taught you along the way. The creative process is a cycle. As you come to the end, the last step helps you begin the process all over again.

After you've savored your cake, take note of what worked well. Take note of things that could have been better. My grandmother has an uncanny ability to take a recipe and tweak it just a little to be even better. Maybe almond extract would be even better than vanilla. Take note of that thought. Take note of what your kids liked. Maybe one element was not as well received. Take note. Maybe something was more difficult than you originally thought. Take note. Last minute substitution fixed a problem? Take note. Ideas sparked for next year or your next event? Pull out your method of taking notes and jot it down.

Keep all those notes handy, because before you can blink an eye, it'll be time to start the process all over with another event or program. You'll be mighty thankful to have those precious tidbits to refer to.

Lucinda Gibson loves serving as the Director of Children's Ministries at FBC Bremen in Bremen, GA. You never know what to expect from her, but you are guaranteed she will be having fun alongside her husband and 3 daughters.

chapter 4

SEEK INSPIRATION

Where to look and what to do

BY BROOKE MILLER

I HAVE HAD SEVERAL FRIENDS over the last few years start in children's ministry and after a few short months find themselves at a loss, some before they even actually started. The complaint I hear most often is that "I'm just not creative." I hate to hear this, but I love to correct it. It's simply not true.

Growing up I always thought that creativity was a characteristic you either have or don't have. Creativity, in my young head, was the ability to paint bright, beautiful watercolors or sculpt realistic designs. My brother and dad were talented artists; I was not. When I began in children's ministry I quickly found out that creativity is more of a fluid scale. It's not limited to mediums we typically think an artist uses. I may not be skilled at drawing, but I have creative solutions to problems. I can't paint, but I can create new games and methods to teach kids. Creativity doesn't

31

present itself in only one channel, which makes it such a powerful and often times overlooked tool.

It's hard to recognize creativity, but it's even harder to cultivate it. Creativity is not often right at your fingertips. It takes time, work, and even practice. The way you flex your creative muscle might be different than the way I do. Nonetheless, I've put together tips to help create an environment that will nurture your creativity:

GET TO A CREATIVE PLACE

If you hit a block, you may just need some inspiration. One of my favorite things to do when I've hit a block is to visit creative environments: theme parks, children's museums, other children's ministries. You might see things you can use in your own context, but more than that, there's something about getting into these creatively charged environments that gives you a new perspective.

A couple years ago I decided to change my typical vacation spot and go to Universal Studios. I was so incredibly inspired by the attention to detail Universal presented to their audience. After returning home I immediately jotted down my notes: what inspired me, what could be duplicated, why it worked. We can learn from the great minds of creativity by visiting inspiring environments.

Children's museums are a fantastic example of this, because everything they create is for the purpose of education and teaching. What better place to gain inspiration than a place with many of the same goals as children's ministries. Take kids to your local children's museum for the day. Watch how they learn, what interests them, and how the museum facilitates that learning.

Visiting different ministries has helped recharge my sense of creativity in the past. If you happen to be near a ministry that is flourishing or maybe a church across town that has a great system that you would like to check out, reach out to the pastor and ask if you can be a fly on the wall. Children's pastors are usually very excited to share with others what they're doing and would happily give you a tour.

If you're unable to physically visit any of these places, consider following them on social media. I follow about a dozen Instagram accounts just because they are creatively different than everyone else. Find some way you can surround yourself with creativity different than your own to challenge yourself.

KEEP A NOTEBOOK

One of the best things that I do to foster creativity in ministry is to keep an ongoing list of ideas. I carry a small notebook with me at all times, but more often than not, I find myself using the notes app in my phone. When you have an idea or are pondering why something is the way it is, stop what you're doing and write it down.

If you don't already do this, stop reading and create a new note in your phone. Anytime you have an idea just write it down. My favorite thing about keeping this note is that it doesn't have to be a fully formed idea. I write down goofy things I think we can do in children's ministry and sometimes after it I write "not sure why," because I've not figured out what it would be used for or even if it would work.

My notes sometimes are a question. When I see the way something functions and wonder why we do it that way or think, "What if we did it another way?" I always write it down to ponder later. I'm not always in position to make changes in the ministry in which I'm working, but by writing it down, I can recall it later when I do have that ability. In six months when I need an outreach idea or a camp theme, I will not have to brainstorm for days and worry about the choice. I have all my ideas in one place.

It seems like a no-brainer, right? Keeping all your ideas in once place is not some mind-blowing, revolutionary idea, but it did revolutionize my creative work. Try doing this for a couple weeks and you'll thank yourself for it later.

KEEP UP WITH THE KIDS

Another fun way to help develop the creative process is to keep up with the kids. Stay in touch with what your kids or the kids in your life are interested in. The easiest way to do this is to hang out with them and take note of things they like. Find out what music, TV shows, and games kids are in to. Be well-versed in the pop culture that kids are interested in. It will give you an edge when you're creating something new and exciting in children's ministry. It's a terrible feeling when you create a curriculum series or VBS theme based on a TV show that was "so last year." Kids are so surprised when adults have watched a show they love or understand how Minecraft works.

One way to conduct your research is following awards shows that are generated by kids voting like the Nickelodeon Kids' Choice Awards and the Radio Disney Music Awards. The Kids' Choice Awards is my favorite because it includes athletes, sports teams, movies, TV shows, music, and even video games. Take some time to check out the nominations and winners of these awards. It may seem silly, but it will give you an idea of what media the kids in your ministry are taking in and how you can use that to your benefit.

Talking to your kids, learning their interests, and experiencing them together should be your primary inspiration. Watch the awards shows together. Have them teach you their favorite trending dance moves. All of these things will help you understand the kids better, but it will also be a source of inspiration for you. You can use the things that they're interested in to help your ministry truly connect with your kids.

PRACTICE CREATIVITY

Daily creative activities will help you cultivate new and exciting brainstorming sessions for your ministry. Writing, sketching, listening, playing music, hiking, and even puzzles are just some of the things you can do to gain inspiration. Even if you're not particularly talented in these areas, just the act is enough. Search for a short writing prompt online and use it to write a story or sketch something that inspires or interests you.

I love this quote by Phil Cousineau, "Inspiration comes and goes. Creativity is the result of practice." Just 10-15 minutes of creative practice each day will grow your creative muscles. Routines are monotonous and don't foster creative thinking. Make sure you're breaking some of your normal routines to help create a space for new ideas. Walk a new path on your way home or have a work meeting outside. Anything different from your normal routine will awaken your right brain as you see and experience different things.

THE PROCESS

The number one thing I always do before a creative session of brainstorming is set up shop. As I previously mentioned, music is a huge source of inspiration for creative work. Sometimes the job calls for jamming out to kids' music; other times I need my own worship music or instrumental to keep me from getting distracted. Playlists like this are available on Spotify and YouTube if you don't feel like making one yourself.

I have a few places between my job and home that I like to work. Before I start working I make sure that the area is clean and organized. If it isn't organized I get distracted from my work by the mess or something else that needs to be taken care of. Bonus points if your work space has a vision board or some other kind of inspiration for you to look at. In addition to choosing music and location, you should unplug if at all possible. Switch your phone to "Do Not Disturb" and turn off your wifi so you don't end up on Facebook or fall into the trap of quickly checking your email. Distractions like this may keep you from your eureka moments when you're creating. For you, setting up shop may mean taking your laptop to the park to work or locking yourself in your office with complete silence.

Remember to take regular breaks when you're working. A technique that I have personally found useful is the Pomodoro. In the Pomodoro technique you set a time for 25 minutes and work the whole time, then take a 5-minute break. Do this four times and after the fourth take a 25- to 30-minute break. You might even have a eureka moment during your break when you take a walk or scroll through Facebook. When I was in college I only allowed myself breaks depending on how much work I got done. For example, I could only go get a snack or drink from the lounge after I had written three full pages of my paper. Whatever method you choose to use, give yourself a break every once in a while.

If you're stuck in your project, try to take a break by doing some monotonous task or activity like taking a walk, washing dishes, or driving. Sometimes, breakthroughs come through shower thoughts. Shower thoughts is the idea that any task that puts you into autopilot is when you are hit with great ideas. I recently realized that I have my own "shower thoughts," sometimes in the shower, but more often in church. Never take your breaks or daily routine for granted as you're working on a creative project.

When you start to work through your ideas you have the opportunity to test and perfect what you've created. The creative process for children's ministers is going to be a little different than that of an artist or a graphic designer. We write, we decorate, we plan events. These things take some testing and rewrites. Unlike artists who may paint and sculpt whatever is in their head without editing or tampering with it, you may need to muddle through your creations. Try out your new ideas and if they don't work, don't be discouraged. Part of being creative and learning creativity is having the courage to try new things. If it fails, tweak it and try again. Brainstorm with your team until you perfect it.

Creativity is such a critical part of what you do in ministering to children. God wired His human creations to be creative but sometimes need an extra push to get going. How inspiring is it to think that the ultimate Creator made us in His image, creativity and all! Be encouraged today. You have been created with the gift of creativity. Try out some new skills and get your creative juices flowing. Remember that everything you do to enhance your creativity will ultimately enhance your ministry and engage the kids in your ministry.

Brooke Miller was born and raised in Indiana but relocated to Seattle in her college years. She is 25 years old, has been doing children's ministry since junior high, and is now an Assembly of God missionary to children in Latin America.

chapter 5

THERE'S A BIG OL' ROCK IN MY WAY

Barriers to creativity

BY JOY CANUPP

"THERE'S NOTHING NEW *under the sun*" (Ecclesiastes 1:9, NIV), yet God has created each person distinctively. He has unique things He wants you to do and create. When you assume you don't have anything to give or can't come up with anything new, you limit your creativity and essentially put God in a small box. Projects, ideas, events, and even thoughts that have occurred in other places by other people can take on your own personal and creative spin.

The barriers to creativity are many. In no particular order, let's explore those and then look at some practical ways to move beyond them. If you truly desire to fulfill all that God intends with your one and only life, you should acknowledge the things that get in the way of your creativity.

PERFECTIONISM

Believing that "perfect" exists is a huge barrier to creativity. I don't want to blindside you here and this may be as devastating as learning that the tooth fairy isn't real, but NOTHING will be perfect this side of heaven. We live in a fallen world and the only perfect person who has ever lived is Jesus. Other than Him, there is not another perfect person or situation or thing or decision or work of art or organization or anything. Perfectionism is only in your imagination (like the tooth fairy). Getting a grasp on this and being okay with it will free you to be more creative.

Practical Perfectionism Busters

- Take note of things in your world that you consider to be excellent. Now, look a little closer and you'll likely find flaws. Be careful not to overuse this exercise to the point of cynicism; but instead, use it to your advantage to see the wonderful in the midst of the non-perfect.

- Have a conversation with someone about your perfectionist tendencies to explore the layers below the surface. This doesn't need to be expensive couch-therapy! Find a trusted person who will keep the conversation focused and will ask good questions to help you look at this area and begin working through it.

FEAR

"Do it scared." You have likely heard that phrase multiple times by now. It has become popular with entrepreneurs, creatives, and the general social media world. Although it has become a common phrase, there is much truth in it. As with most phrases, it's easier to say than to act on. When fear is a barrier to creativity, the best thing that can happen is to take that next step, to push fear aside, and to be creative despite the feelings that are rumbling within.

Practical Fear Busters

- If you like quotes in your work space, put "Do it scared" in a spot where you will see it often. It won't change the world, but it may help shift your inner dialogue.

- Regularly push past fears. What is an activity that you're afraid of? Go do that thing. For me, it's anything dealing with heights, water, or the dark. A few years ago, I ventured out and did a zipline in a dark cavern. Did I love it? Not really. But I lived to tell about it and that has lessened that fear just a bit.

- Make a list of the reasons for your fear in the area of creativity. Read them aloud. Do some of them sound silly? Is it a list you would be willing to share with someone else? Sometimes just getting things out of your head to paper and then aloud is the perspective shift you need.

FATIGUE

Creativity has a hard time competing with fatigue. Most things in life do. Being consistently exhausted is draining and typically puts us in survival mode where creative thoughts are scarce.

Practical Fatigue Busters

- Get more sleep at night.

- Take a mid-day nap.

- Trouble getting that extra sleep at home? Consider checking into a hotel for a good night's sleep, borrow a room at a friend's house while they're on vacation, or sneak away to sack out on the coach in the youth room. Sometimes just a change of environment can give the refreshment needed to bump good sleep habits back in place.

- Move! Walk, jog, bike, anything to get moving. Exercise may seem counter-intuitive, but it is proven to energize and relieve fatigue.

LACK OF MARGIN

For some folks busyness equals importance. When you overextend yourself, your calendar, and the only 24 hours per day that you have, you put yourself in the position of having no margin. No white space. No think time. No moments for creativity. This lack of margin becomes very poor stewardship of your time and buries the creative things that God intends for you to do.

Practical Busters for Margin-less Living

- Schedule meetings with yourself. Seriously! Plan for blocks of time to regularly be alone to think, plan, and create. Write those times on your calendar and stick to them as you would any other important meeting.

- In addition to a couple of hours at a time, a full 2-3 days once or twice a year can be very beneficial. Whether it is designated for a project, long-term planning, or life-planning, the time taken away from normal routine will prove to have multiplied value.

- Take a walk. If you find yourself in the middle of a "meeting-myself-coming-and-going" kind of day, go for a brisk walk. It may be around the parking lot or around the block, but either way, you'll get some fresh air, and that tiny margin in your day can help tremendously.

PROCRASTINATION

Also, a time issue, but in a very different way, is the creative stumbling block called procrastination. In this instance, you have time and often plenty of it, but you choose to put off the task of creating until the last minute. Some folks believe the lie that they are more creative when they work under pressure. Let's just go ahead and call foul on that! The fact is that creating-on-demand because you've waited until the final moments may result in a satisfactory product, but 9 times out of 10, not the best that it could have been if more time was spent in the creating process. In some ways, procrastinating is human nature, but that's not a good enough excuse for it to get in the way of your creativity.

Practical Procrastination Busters

- Set an earlier deadline for yourself. As I'm writing this chapter, I have a submission deadline given to me by my editor friend Tina. For my own purposes ... and so I don't procrastinate ... I've given myself a deadline that is one week earlier. Not only does that provide some margin as mentioned above, it also gives me a reason to celebrate when I finish before the actual date!

- Give yourself small goals within the larger goal. What are the baby steps that need to be taken to get to the end result? Space those out on your calendar appropriately to move you smoothly toward that final date.

- Ask someone to hold you accountable on the small goals and then to celebrate with you when the creative task is completed ahead of schedule.

- Do these things with little and big projects in your life. The more times you finish something well and early, the more you will want to, and the more it will become a habit.

INTERRUPTIONS

Ironically enough, as I am writing this section, a minor situation has occurred causing me to be part of 7 different phone conversations. So, yes, interruptions can greatly interfere with creativity! And those interruptions can come in many forms ... from technology to people to natural causes to car issues to To-Do lists swirling in your head. The key to minimizing this barrier is to acknowledge it and be prepared for it.

Practical Interruption Busters

- Turn off the screens during the creating process.

- Do a "brain dump" in the form of a massive To-Do list and then put it aside. This simple practice will assure your mind that you haven't forgotten anything important, that you will tend to all those things later, and it will allow you to move on with creating!

- Step away from your normal setting if folks around you can't respect your version of a "do not disturb" sign.

LACK OF CONFIDENCE

Do you trust yourself to create? If you just hesitated at all, you may be struggling a bit with this barrier. Lack of confidence hits us all from time to time. And I really mean ALL. Even that guy who looks like he has the world under control—yep, he deals with confidence issues. When it comes to creativity, not being confident in yourself can really get in the way. It can even cause you not to start.

Practical Lack of Confidence Busters

- Read *The Little Engine That Could* by Watty Piper. I'm not even kidding! That fun children's story has a wealth of goodness for adults and a message that you need to be reminded of frequently.

- What is something you don't feel like you're very good at? Write down the reasons why you aren't good at that thing. Now, go chat with a trusted friend. Are your reasons valid or is it a lack of confidence? Sometimes calling out that lack of confidence can be just the confidence-builder you need.

LACK OF STIMULATION

Ever get in a spot where you just feel like things are the "same old, same old"? Being in a rut, looking at the same walls, having the same thoughts, and doing the same schedule day after day can significantly decrease stimulation and therefore creativity.

This one can be particularly easy and fun to overcome. Let's get really practical.

Practical Busters for Lack of Stimulation

- Go to a museum or zoo. No, you don't need to take a kid but you can if you like. Just give yourself a real jolt with the change of scenery.

- Read a book in a category that you typically don't read.

- Go to a store like IKEA where the displays are endless.

- Take a walk in the woods. Take a child and see the world through his little eyes.

- Go to a home improvement store and flip through the hundreds of paint samples. Soak in all the colors. Then go get ice cream (just because).

ISOLATION

Calling all introverts! I can because I am one. This barrier to creativity is one that we are especially susceptible to. Being alone too often and too long can stifle your progress. Creativity needs stimulation and interaction and fresh perspectives. Isolation provides none of these and if it happens for too long can make it even more challenging to bring these things back into your life. I am NOT an advocate for turning introverts into extroverts ... I am saying, though, that your natural preferences are not always healthy for your creativity.

Practical Isolation Busters

- Take a walk with a friend. Being with others doesn't have to equal a big party (sigh of relief from all the introverts). Sometimes just one other person and some good conversation will give you the boost you need.

- Do something fun with your whole family. Being with others also doesn't equal being with a bunch of strangers (another sigh of relief). Plan a fun outing with the people you love the most. Give your brain a chance to rest and focus in other areas. It's very likely that when you return to your creative task you will have a renewed motivation and some fresh perspective.

- Find a place (park, mall, restaurant) where you can make small talk with strangers. I'm pretty sure I just crossed the line with my fellow introverts because even I cringed when I wrote those words! But hang on with me. The fact is, everyone has a story, and those are fun to learn. The trick with this one is to have a couple of good questions to get those stories started and then actively listen. You never know when someone else's story intersecting with your life is going to give your creativity just the boost it needs.

LIFE CRISIS

Life happens. Life does not give you a break when you're working on a creative task. Circumstances, situations, and people can cause interruptions that you never saw coming. When that happens, your creativity can take a hit, be put on pause, or even be halted abruptly for an unknown amount of time. A death in the family will do this. So will a devastated relationship. So will a child going to college. So will a new baby being born. So will a job loss. When (not if) life stuff comes your way, you can decide how to let it affect you. Let's look at this practically. Practical Life Crisis Busters

- Get comfortable with the fact that life will happen to you. You don't have to like it and you certainly don't go looking for it. But when you acknowledge it as part of this journey you are on, it makes it a bit easier when it comes your way.

- Plan for the unknown. That sounds odd. How can you make a plan for something you don't know the details of? This plan is much more internal than external. This plan is giving yourself permission to step back when a life crisis occurs. This plan tells you to give yourself a break when life throws a curveball. This plan says it is okay either to set aside or delegate that creative task while you're putting the pieces of life back together.

- Invite a trusted person to walk this journey with you. You are not created to do life alone. Why do you even try? You are created for community. Whatever that looks like in your life, be sure there is at least one person you can turn to when life hits you hard.

MINDSET

And now we have come full circle ... back to where this chapter started. So many times, your biggest barrier to creativity is right in your own mind. And that is something you get to choose to change!

In this world of instant mashed potatoes and escalators, you need to view creativity as something that takes more time and is done with more effort. There's just nothing like cooking those real potatoes and mashing them the old-fashioned way, leaving chunks, using real cream and lots of love. If creativity could be purchased instantly, everyone would be uber creative, and there would be no need for this chapter. But creativity is not instant, it is not automatic, and it does not come without barriers.

Let's move beyond these barriers and dig deep. Let's know ourselves well and trust the One who created us. Let's go create!

Joy Canupp served as children's minister for 15 years in a SC church and is now encouraging/supporting folks in ministry through retreats, speaking, and blogging at *Leading With Joy* (joycanupp.com). She loves spending time with family and friends, thrifting, playing games, and all things purple!

chapter 6

MIMIC AIRPLANE MODE

Kill procrastination by using your brain

BY JOSH DENHART

ACH DAY YOU APPROACH your goals with great intentions of movement and progress. You desire to move closer to your determined destination and achieve your goals. As you set out on another 8-hour journey, you have grand aspirations of the distance you will travel. You have some vague mental milestones marked out. As you take your first steps on your excursion, you commit to grand outcomes and tell yourself, "Today will be different." But you quickly turn aside and take that well-worn detour into the "Land of Procrastination." This alluring land has many familiar and forbidden destinations: Mt. Gaming, Nap-Ville, The Social Media Forest, and the City of Unnecessary Closet Re-Organization. None of these locations will bring you closer to your goal, but their promise of peace provoke you to pull off the road for just a minute.

When it comes to procrastination, you know the drill all too well. You find yourself spending precious time on lesser things and deep down you hate it. You have an eternal mission but settle for these lesser quick-fix-feel-good alternatives. Though you see the road sign indicating it is just 40 miles to your destination, the colorful billboards invite you to take a break. These off-road excursions inevitably distract and debilitate you. Each time this happens you're wearing a deeper path of purposeless procrastination. Internally, you just want to feel that rush of endorphin-induced accomplishment but, once again, you settle for a short-lived sugar high from the dingy roadside convenience store. Do you even have what it takes to stay on track? In your darker moments, you wonder if you have some low-level version of Adult ADHD. Day after day, you pathetically plod ahead, making meager progress.

This is why Paul the Apostle admonishes us in Ephesians 5:16 (NASB) to *"make the most of the time, for the days are evil."* God knows our proclivity toward procrastination.

If this all-too-common story sadly resonates with you, please understand that you are not alone. Sadly, your experience is quite common. You are not an underachiever. You just need a plan.

Deep within the God-given wiring of your human brain are some little known keys to overcome the pitfalls of procrastination. In this chapter, I'll outline three proven pathways for preventing procrastination.

#1 – END TODAY WITH TOMORROW IN MIND

Have you ever had the experience of not being able to recall the name of a familiar face? We often say, "I can't think of their name. It's on the tip of my tongue!" Soon the conversation moves on as you discontinue seeking to discover that misplaced name. Even though your conscious mind has given up on the search, your deeper subconscious mind has not given up and is now on a mission. In the background, your mind is hard at work, combing through files and folders, looking for the answer to the question your conscious mind just set in motion. Your mind is moving through mountains of minutia, discarding the irrelevant, and honing in on its target. Though the conscious need has passed, your subconscious need has not. The secret search engine of your mind has been powerfully engaged and works on your behalf.

Then, almost magically, in what scientists now call an "Out-of-the-Blue" moment, your brain rejoices and proudly hands you a wrinkled piece of paper with that person's illusive identity identified. Goal achieved! Cognitive dissonance resolved. Endorphins released. Your conscious mind somehow feels a sense of completion as you audibly announce the name that so painfully escaped you earlier.

At this time, the power of your subconscious will pick up yet another task for you and begin to work. This phenomenon of the subconscious is real and powerful. This biological problem solving happens even when you're utterly unaware.

What if I told you that your mind could be working for you even while you sleep? What if I told you that 8 hours of sleep could be positioned to increase your 8 hours of work the next day? Tapping into the subconscious is about working smarter, not working harder.

Your mind has been created to solve problems. Your mind is programmed to keep you safe and sustained as efficiently as possible. Therefore, why not set your subconscious on a secret mission and pre-conquer your tasks for tomorrow? The key to sparking the power of your subconscious is in forcing your mind to work for you in the remote and unrealized realms of the subconscious.

Research shows that by creating tomorrow's To-Do list before you end your work for today, will position you for success. Certainly, you could save yourself 15-20 minutes at the start of your morning if you already had your To-Do list created. However, pre-producing a path for tomorrow's productivity goes much deeper. Predetermining what you want to accomplish tomorrow forces your subconscious to become engaged. Once a set of problems is realized by your conscious mind, your subconscious mind gets right to work, clearing the brush and debris for tomorrow's success. By simply creating your To-Do list at the conclusion of your workday, you can leverage the secret and ever-working subconscious mind on your behalf for a solid 8-12 hours.

Many companies and businesses have virtual employees on the other side of the globe. The employer knows that as the sun is setting in America, the sun is rising in Indonesia. A wise businessperson provides a web-design expert in Indonesia a set of tasks to complete right before heading home from work. The web-coder will start on these tasks about the time the boss's head hits the pillow. When the businessperson arrives back at the office bright and early, the web-coder is just finalizing the task and calling it a day. Pretty cool, huh?

Think of your subconscious as an overseas virtual assistant. This hardworking employee starts their day as you end yours. The key is to provide this eager employee with something substantive to work on while you check out and sleep. Hear this leadership lesson: Your subconscious doesn't sleep.

End today with tomorrow in mind. Create your detailed checklist tonight and unleash the untapped potential of your subconscious mind as you blissfully sleep.

#2 – ENGINEER YOUR BEST ENDORPHIN RUSH

Now that you've set your subconscious mind to work on your behalf, you need to capitalize on the work it has done all night long on your behalf. While you were asleep, your subconscious has been arduously arranging items in your mind and clearing the cognitive clutter so that you can more effortlessly conquer the problem you have set before it. Your mind wants to succeed with the fewest calories burned as possible. You have leveraged the subconscious and now it is time to engage your conscious mind. But there is a problem. Your mind is hungry to feel good. Your mind wants to have a burst of that feel-good hormone: Dopamine. Your body wants that rush.

Do you remember the character Odysseus from Greek mythology? On the journey toward victory, the boats of Odysseus sail dangerously close to the Isle of the Sirens. These mythological temptresses have beautiful songs that lure would-be champions to hear more of their seductive songs, taking them off course and crashing their sea vessels against hidden rocks. The sweet-singing cannibals then devour the would-be heroes. What a tragedy.

Sweet sounding songs tempt us as well. We too turn aside to get a quick fix buzz from social media, obsessively looking to see who liked our meaningless post. We ignorantly get off course and are diverted from the mission as we are lured into just one round of a game on our phone.

It feels good, doesn't it? There's a reason. Your body is releasing dopamine. This powerful substance has been scientifically proven to spike when we use drugs, have sex, check social media, or play a game on our phone. Did you catch that? Brain scans show a spike in feel-good hormones through your harmless use of social media. You just trained your brain where it can get a quick buzz. Need a break? Play a game on your phone. Maybe social media or a game is not as benign as we imagine.

Your brain wants and craves rewards. Your body rewards itself with dopamine. Just like Pavlov's dogs, your body knows that there is a burst of dopamine just waiting on the other side of that Facebook notification glaring at you from your phone. Over time, you will be conditioned to click for that reward.

Just like an untrained child ruins their dinner by gorging themselves on candy, the song of the Sirens seduces us, too. We take the bait. We crash into the underwater rocks. We ruin our productivity. We took the lesser buzz.

In Homer's story of Odysseus, there was another character, Jason. He too faced the temptation of the Sirens. But his solution was a different order. Jason declined to plug the ears of his crew like Odysseus. Instead, he ordered Orpheus, a musician of incomparable talent, to play his most beautiful songs. The Sirens didn't stand a chance! Jason and his men were not in the least inclined to succumb. Why? They rebuffed the sounds of the Sirens because they had heard something far better.

We need to retrain our system. We need to listen for a better song. We need to hold out for the bigger buzz. You want to feel good. You must train your body and mind to hold out for the greater feel-good moment.

In his best selling book, *Deep Work*, Cal Newport decries the sad state of our digitally addicted society. Using hard-won scientific research, Newport shows how digital distractions short-circuit our ability to concentrate. This creates a cyclical pattern of taking the quick-fix buzz time and time again.

But deeper work creates a better buzz. Deep work creates deeper rewards biologically as well as professionally. This skill takes practice, however. You need to resist the instant-yet-short-lived dopamine rush that comes from checking your device. Then you can train your body's reward center to kick out those feel-good hormones as you come up for air after a 2-hour session of deep and undistracted work. Deep work takes deep concentration and provides deep rewards.

When you achieve something of significance, you will be rewarded with dopamine. You will not only have a natural high, you will be moving toward your goal and you can begin to rewrite what your brain craves. A snowball affect starts to takes place. At first, your body feels deprived as you detach and double-down. However, if you stay focused, listening to the right song, you will set new reward patterns and the body will want more.

Dopamine is addictive. You just need to train your brain where you can get the most dopamine. Trust me, your body will respond. And if you don't trust me, trust the overwhelming scientific evidence of brain chemistry.

Engineer your best endorphin rush. Don't ruin your dinner with a lesser buzz. Hold out and create a new pathway.

#3 – AMAZING ACHIEVEMENTS THROUGH AIRPLANE MODE

So far, we have discussed the brain research surrounding the subconscious mind. In addition, we delved into the scientific data surrounding pleasure centers of the brain and dopamine. Now it's time to leave the theoretical and move to the practical. It's time to explore some practical steps to defeat procrastination and increase productivity.

As I write this chapter, I am sitting on an airplane. I have my phone in "airplane mode." It's impossible for me to be interrupted by my phone. I'm wearing noise-canceling headphones. These advanced headphones stop certain frequencies from getting through to my ears. In addition, I have to use the bathroom. That's right. I need to use the restroom right now. However, I'm not allowed to stand up and move freely at this point of the flight. So, I will hold it and keep working.

I get so much done on an airplane. What's so unique about being on an airplane that dramatically increases my productivity? I believe it's because certain conditions have minimized distraction.

John Acuff wrote a bestselling book entitled *Finish*. He sets forth a compelling case for how to carry an important task through to completion and finish. Acuff reminded me how much I got done when I was on an airplane. But he pushed deeper and challenged me to mimic the conditions of being on an airplane in my regular and daily life.

I took up the challenge and I started replicating the conditions I experienced on an airplane for two hours at the start of each day. I put on the headphones, put my phone on do not disturb, and work diligently. When I came up for air after working hard for two, uninterrupted hours, I realized that no national emergencies had occurred and no one had needed me. Novel thought.

Acuff's observation of airplanes, coupled with Cal Newport's insistence that devices doom our ability to deliver, I decided to take some radical but practical changes. Brace yourself.

First, I deleted Twitter from my phone. Next, I deleted LinkedIn from my phone. I deleted all news apps like CNN or FOX News. These items were distractions and were not delivering any real value to me or my goals.

I took it to a deeper level when I entered the "Notifications" area of my iPhone X. I disabled notifications for Instagram and email. Yes, if someone emailed me, my phone would not vibrate and it would not make a dinging noise.

I removed notifications on my phone from Facebook. I would no longer see a tempting red number "5" telling me that five people had liked a photo of my son riding his bike. This was nothing but a potential distraction.

I deleted the one and only game on my phone: Hay Day. This super-addictive farming game was a monumental time waster that I felt I deserved as a harmless way to relax. But who was I fooling? At the slightest moment of boredom, I whipped out my phone and did a "little farming." Then I noticed I had a Facebook notification and several emails. And just like that, I rammed my productivity vessel into the hidden rocks as carnivorous cannibals scarfed down my precious time. Just as the mythological victims of Homer's story were oblivious to how far they had strayed, you too can lose track of how much time has elapsed through one simple digital detour.

I deleted some stuff and stopped alerts. Interestingly enough, I have survived. It took a week or two to recondition myself from instinctively grabbing my phone for a quick buzz. I still check email and Facebook, yet just on my terms.

THE CONCLUSION AND CHALLENGE

Your subconscious is eager to produce for you. Try ending today with tomorrow in mind. Make your list tonight and watch tomorrow soar.

Your body craves feeling good. Try engineering your endorphin rush and holding out for a greater dose of dopamine.

Here is the greatest challenge: Mimic the conditions you experience on an airplane. There are truly amazing achievements to be had through airplane mode.

Take on procrastination with some solid brain research and conquer your creative dreams.

As a former high school chemistry teacher and full-time children's pastor, **Josh Denhart** melded his love for science and Christ by creating The Amazing Chemistry Show, a traveling, Gospel-centered stage show with fire, explosions, and foam. Carrying his ministry of chemistry even further, Josh has created 3 Science VBS curricula, a family science devotional, a school day STEM program, ministry training materials, and he regularly hosts a "wacky science" spot on his local TV station's morning program.

chapter 7

CREATIVITY BEGETS CREATIVITY

10 creativity exercises to try

BY ANGELA SANGALANG

A KIDMIN VOLUNTEER ALWAYS lamented and apologized to me for not being a creative person. Despite being an amazing leader who loved the children, showed up to every meeting, and used her own money for the ministry, she didn't think she was making enough of an impact in kidmin because she didn't see herself as a creative person.

In Exodus 35:30-35, Moses turned to the Israelites and pointed out two men, Bezalel and Oholiab, who were wildly creative. They made artistic designs on different mediums; they worked with stone, wood, and fabric; and they were engravers, designers, embroiderers, and weavers. They also had wisdom, understanding, knowledge, and all kinds of skills. They even had the ability to teach others. Raise your hand if you would recruit these guys for the ministry. I would!

Despite how creative Bezalel and Oholiab were, Moses said something about them that is more important than their talents and skills. Moses said that the Lord chose them, *"filled them with the Spirit of God,"* and *"filled them with skill to do all kinds of work"* (Exodus 35:31 & 35, NIV).

God chose and filled them. That's the most important thing Moses said about those men. That's the most important thing you can remember when it comes to creativity. God chose and filled you with all the skills you could ever need to do His work here on earth. That includes creativity! Your job now is to use it.

Steven Pressfield wrote in *The War of Art* that creative work is, "a gift to the world and every being in it. Don't cheat us of your contribution. Give us what you've got."

As with any skill, you need to practice creativity. You need to exercise your creative muscles because creativity begets creativity. The more you practice being creative, the better you get at it. The difference with this skill is that anything goes. There are many ways to be creative!

In children's ministry, creativity doesn't just belong in making crafts or in stage design. You can be creative in how you schedule volunteers so every role is covered. You can be creative in making your budget stretch. You can be creative in how you present the Gospel, welcome guests, take up offering, announce events, and everything in between.

You just need to figure out how to inject creativity into those different areas. Remember, God chose and filled you. You just need to use the creativity already in you. Here are 10 creativity exercises you can try that will inspire you, motivate you, and help you look at creativity in different ways.

#1. PRAY AND READ THE BIBLE IN A NEW WAY.

Let's start with something you already do—praying and reading the Bible. How do you pray? How do you read the Bible? For a week, change your routine. Pray differently. Read your Bible differently. Check out these ideas.

1. Write, draw, paint, or sculpt your prayers.
2. Turn your prayer into a vision board.
3. Make a scrapbook of your prayers.
4. Make a collage representing a key Bible verse.
5. Turn a Scripture passage into a poem or a song.
6. Try Bible journaling.

#2. PRAISE GOD WITH A HAIRBRUSH.

Remember your teenage years? You're alone in your room, the music is blaring, and your hairbrush becomes a microphone or a guitar. Creativity isn't just a mental muscle. It's physical, too. Get up, grab a hairbrush, put on your favorite upbeat praise song, and rock on!

You can do this with a spatula while you cook dinner, with a broom while you sweep the floor, or with whatever is on hand while you go about your day. It may seem silly, but the more you do it, the more you'll lose self-consciousness. Come Sunday morning, you can show the kids how they can praise God with everything they've got.

#3. WATCH A DISNEY LIVE ACTION PRODUCTION.

This is my favorite creativity exercise and one that I think you'll love. Disney is amazing at turning any space or stage into a whole new world (pun intended). I'm always inspired by how they work with what they've got. Watching a Disney live action production helps me look at our ministry space differently. It helps me see how I can give our families a safe and inviting space where they can meet Jesus. Watch a Disney production and let their creativity inspire yours.

#4. LEARN AN ART SKILL IN PERSON.

Whether it's a recipe, a dance choreography, or changing a flat tire, if something is intimidating, break it down into smaller, do-able steps. Art is the same way. Many people find it intimidating, which is why if they can't draw, paint, or sculpt, they think they're not creative. However, art can be broken down into smaller, doable steps. For example, to draw a person, you first draw a bunch of shapes like squares, triangles, rectangles, and circles. Think of them as building blocks that you shape and refine.

With this creativity exercise, you will need to find an artist. Look around in your church. There's probably at least one person who can draw, paint, or sculpt. Ask him/her to teach you to do one thing like draw a tree, paint a rock, or sculpt clay into a vase. Learn how she breaks down the process into smaller, doable steps. Follow his example, and you'll see how you can create a masterpiece. If you can't find such a person, look for local paint parties where everyone gets a canvas, paint, and directions from an instructor.

The next time you're staring at a ministry project that requires a lot of creativity, remember to break it down into smaller, doable steps.

#5. ATTEND AN ART FESTIVAL.

Paul warns us, *"Do not be misled: Bad company corrupts good character"* (1 Corinthians 15:33, NIV). Good character, therefore, encourages good character. This is why people exercise together to pursue a healthy lifestyle or join books clubs to read more books. Surround yourself with people who have the character, lifestyle, or skills you wish to have yourself.

Art festivals ooze creativity. To exercise your creative muscles, attend an art festival. Look at art. Feel it. Hear it. Try it. Enjoy it. Surround yourself with creativity. Immerse yourself in it. Chat with artists and ask what inspires them. Participate in any hands-on activities. Find an art piece that intrigues you and purchase it.

In the wilderness, animals flock to a watering hole to quench their thirst. If you're feeling creatively dry, go someplace full of it. If there are no art festivals going on, find an art museum to wander through.

#6. ASK A CHILD TO TELL YOU A STORY.

Children are very creative. This is something we know in kidmin! Their imaginations run wild with ease, something that adults sometimes struggle with. Most of them also like to talk, especially when they have your undivided attention. Find a child and ask him to tell you a story. It can be any story! It can be true or made up. It can be about what she did yesterday or about a favorite toy.

Enjoy the story, but also pay attention to the child's line of thinking. See how one idea leads to another, and another, and another. This is creativity at work! Now, I have to warn you that this creativity exercise can be time-consuming. Who knows how long a child's story will be! It's also totally worth it, because time spent with a child is precious.

#7. RETELL A BIBLE STORY FROM A DIFFERENT PERSPECTIVE.

There's a Sunday school song about Jesus walking on water that goes like this:

I saw footprints on the water, footprints on the sea
Footprints on the water, I could not believe
I saw Jesus, Jesus, walking on the waves
Footprints on the water that day.

("Footprints On The Water", Words & Music by Stephen Elkins)

Can you tell who is singing the song? It's a fish! The writer took a familiar Bible story and retold it from the perspective of a fish. Why don't you do the same? Pick your favorite Bible story or the one you're going to teach next Sunday and retell it from the perspective of a different character. This will not only exercise your creativity, it could also breathe new excitement for the Bible into you and your kids.

8. TRY YOUR HAND AT IMPROV.

One of the most fun and creative ways I've taught a Bible story is through improv. After telling my group the story, I give them different roles and tell them to act it out. I turn on the camera and let them have the stage. Since my group consists of 5- and 6-year-olds, I'm always stuck as the narrator. Instead of reading straight from the Bible, I retell the story with as much emotion as possible. I may even add a gasp here and there.

Improv puts people on the spot. Why not jump into the spotlight alongside them. Film your efforts and show it to the parents, post it online (on your private ministry page, of course), and share it with your pastors and church leaders.

What I love about this creativity exercise is it makes the Bible memorable for kids and gives you an opportunity to share with others what you're doing in kidmin. Hint: it's a great recruitment tool and budget booster, also!

#9. TEACH TO DIFFERENT LEARNING STYLES.

You might already know about the different learning styles, but allow me to refresh your memory. Every person learns differently. Many sources cite seven learning styles, which are: visual, auditory-musical, verbal, physical, logical, social, and solitary. You have your preferred learning style, but you also have your preferred teaching style. These two may not be similar.

Exercise your creative muscles by teaching to these different learning styles. If you love to use pictures, use music. If you love group work, try individual work. Play a game. Ask analytical questions. Talk more. Talk less.

Teach in different ways. Step out of your comfort zone in order to get creative. Doing this doesn't just benefit your creativity. It will help your kids learn with their preferred learning styles, and it will help you become better at teaching the Gospel effectively.

#10. DEVIATE FROM ROUTINE.

Routine is great with children when you're talking about schedules and forming good habits. Routine is amazing when it helps you stay organized and on time. However, routine can also send you into a stalemate when you become too comfortable. It can cause you to plateau in your leadership effectiveness.

You may have sensed a theme in these creativity exercises. It's to do something different. Change things up. Deviate from routine. Synonyms of creativity include inventiveness, originality, and innovation. Creativity requires you to step aside from the tired and old.

With this last creative exercise, look at the different routines in your life: the roads you take to and from work; the recipes you use every week; the games you play in kidmin; the people you talk to after church. Look at them and deviate.

Take a different route to work. Stop by a park on the way home. Try a new recipe from a country you've never visited. Play new games. Talk to other people. Consult with Pinterest for bucket list activities and social media challenges.

Deviate from routine and see what happens. Change things up to spark your creativity. Step aside from the tired and old and step into inventiveness, originality, and innovation.

Maya Angelou said, "You can't use up creativity. The more you use, the more you have." Try one, two, or all of these creativity exercises, and allow the God-given creativity to flow out of you, expand around you, and inspire those who meet you. Remember, God chose and filled you. Give us what you've got!

Angela Sangalang is a Family Ministry Director in San Jose, CA, and writer of kidmintogether.com. She can be bribed with coffee, chocolate, and yarn. (She'll knit you a scarf if you ask nicely.)

chapter 8

THEMES, LISTS, AND COFFEE
The evolution of a project

BY CORINNE NOBLE

I ALWAYS LOVE A NEW kids' ministry project to sink my creative teeth into. There arc many projects you take on as ministry leaders. You plan everything from events, offering contests, and camps, to curriculum, services, and VBS. A lot of what you do in your ministry requires you to think creatively and come up with new and innovative ideas. Your ideas are constantly changing throughout each project. In fact, by the time you're done with a project it might not even look like what you started with. That's because creative thinking evolves over the time it takes to finish a project.

A JUMPING-OFF POINT

Before you can get your creative juices flowing, every project needs a jumping-off point or springboard. You may want to start with a biblical passage, a topic, or a theme. It depends on the project, but my favorite springboard is typically a theme.

A great theme will get your brain thinking so quickly that you won't be able to write the ideas down fast enough. I recently decided on my theme for writing next year's VBS and ideas were coming to my brain hours later. I'm sure you can think of a time when you were planning a project and came up with a theme that inspired you to the core. When you find a theme, topic, or biblical passage that inspires you to that level, you know you've found the perfect springboard for your project.

GIVE IT SOME TIME

Never wait until the last minute to start planning! Though you can come up with creative ideas quickly or at the last minute, it's much more productive to give your creative process time to grow and evolve. Ideas are like plants—they need to be nurtured and given time to grow and blossom to their full potential. Good ideas morph into great ideas when you give them enough time to mature. When you come up with an idea for an upcoming project, write it down with as much additional information as possible. This will make your future planning easier. Once you've dumped all your ideas onto a piece of paper or document on your computer, walk away from it for a little while. The length of time can depend on your project due date. Put the project on a back burner in your brain until you come up with even more ideas to dump in the same list. Repeat this process until you're closer to the project deadline or have compiled an adequate list of ideas to start fleshing them out.

LISTS, LISTS, AND MORE LISTS

In my opinion, you can never have too many lists with a project. Lists do so many wonderful things! I make lists to brainstorm ideas and make sure I don't forget anything. Lists actually help me sleep at night, and they move the creative thinking process along. When you keep all your ideas for a project crammed in your brain, it can drive you out of your mind. The ideas spiral around in your head, you worry about forgetting them, and you make mental lists over and over. Get out a pen and paper or your favorite note-taking software and start writing your ideas down! I've always been a huge fan of writing things down in a notebook, but sometimes notebooks get lost or left at the office when you really need them at home. I have recently shifted to using Microsoft OneNote for all of my lists and I will never turn back. I have all my lists in one place and they sync between my phone, tablet, laptop, and desktop. Now, any time I get a creative idea about a project, I can throw it in the appropriate notebook inside OneNote.

BRAINSTORMING TIME

I love making brainstorming lists for my projects. It's fun to see where an idea began and how much it changes through the brainstorming process. I usually begin by writing down different themes or names for the project. Once I have 5-10 ideas, I choose my favorite theme from the list. Then, I create a list of all the elements I want to include and their quantities. For example: 3 games, 1 skit, 2 crafts, 1 Bible story, 2 video clips, 6 verses, 2 snacks. Once the list of elements is complete, create a separate brainstorm list for each element. This may seem like a lot of lists, but you will be thankful for them when it's time to execute the project. Look at the quantity of each element and give yourself a few extra ideas in case you end up discarding some of them later. Your brainstorming lists are never set in stone and you don't have to stick directly to them, but they're a great place to get started and help move the creative process along.

WRITE IT OUT

While I would love to live in the brainstorming phase of a project forever, that's only the beginning of the creative process. Once your lists have more than enough ideas to make your project happen, it's time to start writing out your elements. Some people prefer to skip this step before execution, but

I strongly advise against it. While you are fleshing out each element, you might find that some of your ideas don't sound as good as they did during the brainstorming session. Many times, you'll find yourself making additions to your original ideas as you write out the details. Writing it out forces you to think through each step of execution to make it more effective and fun for the kids and your team. As you write, envision where the kids will stand, what distance is a reasonable toss, how everything fits into the space, and when each step happens. This step of writing it down can easily be the difference between a successful activity or a chaotic one.

EXECUTE THE PROJECT

The creative process is not over once the planning is complete. It continues into the execution stage of the project. As you execute, you will tweak your ideas to make them fit the allotted time as well as the specific audience. Creative ideas will often come to me when I'm already on a stage or speaking to kids. There's a fine line between boxing yourself in to your plan and throwing it out completely. Allow yourself space to be creative and make it your own. I've seen many games and object lessons that looked great on paper, but for some reason just fell flat in the execution. You must be able to think on your feet and turn the situation around on the fly, if necessary. If a volunteer or a team of volunteers are helping you execute the project, give them the ability to add their creative touch to whatever they're leading. Different people will bring their own unique ideas and style to the exact same thing if they are given the permission to do so.

THE AFTERMATH

Many of the projects you take on in kids' ministry will be re-executed in some way. You may do VBS, camp, a lock-in, a worship night, and weekly services every year. That means the creative thinking process doesn't end when your current project is in the rearview mirror. Get out that notebook again and write down all the positive things about the project.

- What did the kids love?
- What were the leaders excited about?
- What went better this time than the last time you completed a similar project?

This list will be the first thing you look at the next time you plan a similar project. Writing it down assures that you don't forget those elements. Then, make the list that's a little less pleasant, but really needed.

- What are the things that went wrong?
- What could have been done differently?
- What bored the kids to death?
- What made your leaders want to tear their hair out?

This list will encompass all of the things you want to avoid or do differently next time you execute the project. Last, make the best list of all.

- What can I do to make this project even better next time?
- What new goals can we set that will stretch us?

Each time you do an event, service, or anything else in your ministry, you should always strive for it to be an improvement and build on what you've learned. Making these lists will make the next time you do a project much easier.

EXAMPLES OF THE EVOLUTION

I love seeing my ideas change and grow from a tiny idea to full-blown event. One of my favorite things to do in kids' ministry is to write curriculum, but there are a lot of steps required to plan a new series. I might begin with the idea to do a glow-in-the-dark series (the springboard), but I'm not sure what scripture passages to cover in the series. I look through my Bible, pray, do some google searches, ask some people I know, and

INSPIRED: UNLOCKING YOUR CREATIVITY

write down any passages that stick out to me that might go with the theme.

I will also need a title for my series, so I'll make a list of all the different titles I can think of until I settle on the one I like the most. The title I choose might affect the passage of scripture I use for the series or vice-versa. Once I have my theme, title, and scripture passages, I write down all of the elements I want to include. Most of my curriculum series include skits, Bible stories, verses, object lessons, games, small group time, and review.

Next, I make brainstorming lists for each of the elements I just listed with a few extra ideas in each list. Then, I outline each week of the series by placing the elements from each of my brainstorming lists into each week. I may decide to change some of the games or object lessons at this point, because I'm digging deeper into the theme of each week. Finally, I write out each element individually to create the curriculum for the week.

VBS is another example of a project the requires a lot of creative thinking. I start thinking about next year's VBS before this year's VBS is over. VBS is one of those events that needs the largest amount of time possible to develop and plan. I choose my theme (the springboard) for VBS about a year in advance. Then, I begin my first list of ideas and Pinterest board. I continue to add to that first list every time I get a new idea for the next 6 months. About 6 months before the event, I begin my brainstorming lists for environments, small group rotations, and services. Three months before the event, I take my brainstorming lists, narrow them down to the elements I'm going to use, and begin writing it out to create the curriculum. Two months before VBS, I make lists of all the things I need to buy and create. Over the remaining 8 weeks, I continue to add to the list of ideas for the environments and services as they continue to come to me. Finally, I execute as many of the ideas on my list as possible, forcing myself to let go of some of the less important ones because of time constraints. Following VBS, I make my lists of all the things that went well, things to do differently, and ways to make it even better next year.

So many things will change and evolve between my initial idea and the final product. That's the beauty of the creative process when you give yourself the time to allow it to work. Don't try to contain your creativity in last year's box. You should think of creativity as a liquid, not a solid. You must give your creative thinking the space and time it needs to flow and change. Now, get out there and create something new!

Corinne Noble is the Children's Pastor at Desert Springs Church in Chandler, AZ. She received her call to kids' ministry when she was only 10 years old, and has been involved in kids' ministry ever since. She enjoys writing curriculum, creating set designs, and sharing her ideas with other kids' ministry leaders. When she's not doing ministry, she loves to cook, bake, and spend time with her husband, Sean.

chapter 9

MUSICAL CHAIRS

A lesson in adaptability, preparedness,
and risk taking

BY ANNA SMALLEY

D ay 2 of camp. The plan is simple.

- Breakfast
- Large group
- Activities: zipline, archery, GaGa Ball tournament, or swimming

The plan is for 75 campers to rotate through two of these activities over the course of the day with lunch in between. Just as campers are heading to the dining hall for lunch a torrential downpour begins. I don't mean like a bunch of rain falling from the sky; I mean like poor Ms. Karen was drenched to her bones as she ran the 100 feet from her cabin to the dining hall door. With each step, water squirted out the front end of the kids' shoes. How does this happen? Of all the days in summer, the floodgates open the one day we have planned to be outside all day long.

I sat down to lunch with my soggy wet staff. They looked at me and said, "What now?" I needed a plan. The forecast called for rain the rest of the afternoon. We had to do something. I didn't have much for extra supplies. I didn't want to just plop them in front of a movie, so I went with the first thing that came to mind: musical chairs.

I know, a book on creativity and here I am telling you that the best rain day plan is musical chairs!

Here's the thing. We played musical chairs—leaders and kids alike—for over two hours. We belly laughed. We raced around chairs. We let kids pick the songs. (To my surprise they asked if I could play the "Fresh Prince of Bel Aire Song" and, of course, I said yes.) At the end of camp when we asked kids to identify their favorite part, over and over the resounding answer was "musical chairs."

Someone very wise once told me, "You better have a plan B. If you don't, the kids will!" The staff I work with probably thinks this phrase is my ride or die. On occasion when really big events are coming up I add to it. "You better have a plan B, C, D, E ... you know what I mean!"

I think in kids' ministry we'd all like to think we're pretty quick on our toes. If the glue doesn't hold the cotton ball on, it's okay. You've got glue dots! You forgot the scissors? No big deal! You'll teach kids to fold and tear. A volunteer calls out with food poisoning? It's not ideal, but you can combine two age groups and make it work for today. But what happens when something really truly blindsides you? What happens when even those seasoned in ministry are stumped? How do you dig yourself out of an unexpected hole and not just get by, but succeed?

FLEXIBLE AS A WET SPAGHETTI NOODLE

There's much to be said about flexibility and adaptability. Youth pastors are notoriously good at this. Oftentimes, kids' pastors who are known for being programmed, organized, scheduled, and coordinated look at youth pastors and mistake their adaptability for a lack of preparation, but the truth is, many youth pastors are gifted at looking at a situation and seeing five different ways to tackle it head on. You can learn something from them. You can't be so convinced that if Plan A fails Plan B will succeed. You probably know as well as I do that many factors play into success. There's the weather, and the volunteers, and the space, and the money, and the kids, and the supplies, but it's so important that you not get so wrapped up in your own plans that you miss the things that are right in front of you.

Jesus got this! In Mark 6 Jesus is preaching to the crowd that's gathered on a hill. It's late in the afternoon and people are getting hungry.

Jesus' disciples are noticing a problem.

"'Send the crowds away so they can go to the nearby farms and villages and buy something to eat.'

But Jesus said, 'You feed them.'

'With what?' they asked. 'We'd have to work for months to earn enough money to buy food for all these people'" (Mark 6:36-37, NLT).

These guys were in the same shoes you and I have been in many times. They went to Jesus expecting Him to just handle it and He turned it back on them. "You feed them." This is where my teenage self (and sometimes my 31-year-old self) wants to roll my eyes as I huff and puff that it wasn't my fault, so I shouldn't have to fix it! But Jesus didn't just leave them hanging. He pointed out the start to a solution.

"'How much bread do you have?' he asked. 'Go and find out'" (Mark 6:38, NLT).

The men did some investigating and found they had some bread and some fish. Though it wasn't enough, it didn't have to be. They also had Jesus. He took the little bit they were able to find and did something miraculous with it. And that wasn't a one-time deal, folks. When you find yourself in a situation that feels as if it's spiraling out of your control you need to step back and take a look around. Grab onto something—anything that looks like it might work, then turn it over to Jesus. He can make baskets of bread where you saw only a handful.

Now don't stop reading here. This whole book is about creativity and some of you are saying, "All she told me was to pray. Obviously, I'd pray! I need to know how to creatively problem solve." But I listed this one first on purpose. So often when I find myself backed up against the wall I look first to me, myself, and I to see what can be done before ever asking how God would like to use me in the situation. Be flexible and allow Jesus to do something great through you.

CREATIVE PROBLEM SOLVING FOR DUMMIES

So much of problem solving has to do with preparedness. Thinking through several possibilities for each situation you may encounter will often serve you very well.

If you're a Type A like me you research something, make lists of supplies, check it twice and three times, prep the supplies, and you're ready to go. Everything has a purpose. But what if everything doesn't have a purpose but rather many purposes? It's easy to get so caught up in the way it's supposed to work that you can't see any other possibility. I'd encourage you to start seeing things for more than what they are at face value. A package of Oreos may be the intended snack. But it's also a game. (Take the cream out of all of them and make a stack of creams to see how big of an Oreo you can make.) Or, make a competition where you stick one on each kid's forehead and tell them they have one minute to get it in their mouth without using their hands. You could have a contest where you stack the cookies on the end of a popsicle stick hanging out of a kid's mouth and have them see how many they can stack.

Viewing things with more than one possible use comes in handy when you find yourself in a bind.

But this doesn't just happen with supplies. We all know it happens with volunteers, too! I encourage my staff all the time to think through other options when they're leaving the office at the end of the week with 10 holes in the Sunday schedule. What age groups can be combined? Who have they not asked yet? Could someone swap weeks or service times or classrooms to fill a gap? Have they reached out to the subs every way possible in an attempt to get a response? Are there other church staff who might be available to fill in? If they spend time investing in plans B, C, and D, Sunday morning suddenly feels a little less stressful. They know what the options are and several possible solutions are in their back pocket ready to be put into play if necessary.

And when it's not supplies or volunteers, it's the people you serve that shake things up, or the money in your budget (or not in your budget), or the space you have at the church. I strongly encourage you to regularly evaluate everything. Just because it's working now doesn't mean it's the very best option. And just because it's the very best option now doesn't mean it's going to be in three months.

Creativity can take time. It rarely happens on the fly. Allow yourself time to research and investigate, and develop several different options so that when you're confronted with something less than ideal you've already got wheels in motion.

THROW IT TO THE WALL AND SEE WHAT STICKS!

"If you're going to risk and maybe fail, fail at something that matters. Fail gloriously so that even in failure, lives change."
–Jon Acuff

The most creative people I know are giant risk takers. If you're already worried that you're just not cut out for that, it's okay! That's where the adaptability thing is going to come into play.

When I entered ministry, I put my head down and worked hard. I was determined that everything we did to draw kids closer to Jesus would be the very best. It was my dedication to doing things this way that actually led me to take my first real big risk in ministry. I was an intern at a growing church in Omaha, NE and the kids' pastor was interested in offering an on-site evening PreK/K camp for the first time ever. It would run at the same time as the sports camp offered for elementary kids. The catch was there was no money to buy additional curriculum for the PreK/K kids and the sports camp curriculum was just too far above their heads. I spent days researching old Sunday school and VBS curriculum and just wasn't satisfied with anything. Enter my first big risk: I approached Sandy, my leader, and said, "I think our best option here is for me to write the curriculum." I was 22. I'd just finished school. I'd never written an entire week of curriculum for anything before. And for some reason, she trusted me with it. I poured hours into the camp. We were thrilled with the outcome and have offered a PreK/K option every year since.

I had no idea if it was going to work, but I was willing to try. The possible reward was worth the risk.

I tell my team all the time, "Let's give it a shot. If it doesn't work or we don't like it, we don't ever have to do it again." I would never have had that mentality 10 years ago. I'd have much preferred to play it safe for fear that I'd upset someone or something or some system that had been in place for years. But there is so much potential in the risk!

What things would you do differently if you knew there was no possibility it could fail? What programs would you start or end? Who would you recruit to serve? How would you create spaces for kids to bump elbows with Jesus? These are exactly the kinds of questions to think through as you stretch and grow in your creativity.

And if it's all still so intimidating, start small. Let one of those risky dreams out of the bag. Communicate up well. Get your leadership on board. Communicate down just as well. Gain buy-in from those who serve under your leadership. You're really casting vision for your risk. Continue to reiterate the vision every step of the way. The likelihood is, your risk will pay off if you've planned it out well and given it the time and attention it deserves.

My husband would tell you I like to play it safe. That is true in almost every aspect of my life. But when it comes to ministry, when it comes to leading kids to Jesus, I find that I have a tremendous amount of courage to do whatever it takes to get them as close to Him as possible. Creative problem solvers take risks.

MUSICAL CHAIRS

Our little game of musical chairs would've been just okay on its own. It would've kept kids entertained and active but that's not why it was successful. It was successful because we took something familiar to kids and blew it up on a grander scale. (Nearly 100 people played the same game at the same time.) It was successful because we allowed our campers to have a voice in the game. (They got to select the music that was played.) It was successful because it was two hours in an enclosed space where they could form relationships with their leaders and other campers. It was successful because we looked around at what we had, saw it wasn't much but went for it anyway, trusting that God would take care of the rest.

Friends, you don't have to be the most creative person in the room to be a great problem solver. Be adaptable and let Jesus use what you've got. Come prepared and be ready to view things for all they could be rather than what you'd hoped they'd be. And step out in faith, even just a little. You never know where that little risk will lead you.

***

Aanna Smalley has been in kidmin for 10 years (which means she still has plenty to figure out!) She loves Jesus, family, coffee, and Jazzercise!

chapter 10

KNOCK, KNOCK

Invite God into your creative process

BY ELLEN HALEY

Knock, knock.

Oh, no! There wasn't time for this?

It was easy to recognize the strong but sure knock.

A voice on the other side called out softly, "CM (Children's Minister)? You missed our meeting this morning." Pause, and then the voice repeats, "CM?"

From inside the room, the CM groaned," Oh no. It's the boss, the senior pastor. There's too much to do. This project has to be ready this afternoon."

"Besides," CM thinks, "Why did they need to get together to work on the project? They hired me because of my talents and abilities."

If there was no response, hopefully, he would go away and CM could get focused back on all there was left to do. Then later there would be time to bring the work to the boss, showing what CM had done for him.

Knock, knock.

After another pause, knock, knock, knock. Another minute later, steps could be heard returning down the hallway.

Alone.

W OULD YOU DO THIS with your senior pastor or with any other boss? Or for that matter, would anyone do this with their secular supervisor? No? Then why do you, at times, do this to God ... closing yourself off, focusing on whatever your latest creative project is, confident in your own abilities, too busy to take the time to invite Him into your creative process.

Why do so many of you create all these exciting events, write insightful blogs, creatively solve ministry problems, pen amazing and awesome curriculum using the creativity that God has given you, and then only after it (whatever "it" is) take it to God and say, "Here, look what I've done for You. Here You go. Can You bless it?"

Bobbi Harrison (Apostolic Revival Center in Peru, IN) stated it this way, "Too often we ask God to bless what we are doing, when we should be asking God to help us do what He's blessing."

You fail to invite God into your creative process. Even from far away I can hear the voices, "But I'm doing it for Him." Think about that. Who is the emphasis on? Who garners the glory? Is the creative work solely for Him, for God's glory and God's kingdom? Or is it because you want to do it and you seek the glory and accolades.

We all do it at some time, whether out of an inability to surrender control or it's just easier. Or perhaps it's to focus attention on ourselves. This brings to mind King Saul, impatiently waiting for the prophet Samuel to arrive, decided to offer the burnt offering himself (1 Samuel 13:6-15). On the surface, his intent was good and the burnt offering being lifted would have been pleasing to God but ... it was not God's will and God 's way. Saul kept in control and left God out, hoping God would bless it. That didn't turn out so well for Saul in the end. Jonah tried to go his own way and Peter tried to walk on water but then took his eyes off Jesus.

When you take your eyes off God and don't take the time to include Him in your creative activity you ultimately lose sight of what you're doing. Although it may turn out great on the surface, whatever your creative work is ultimately leaves a void once the earthly satisfaction has faded. But what can you do? What should you do?

Let's imagine this scenario instead.

CM sits waiting, yes impatiently, but like that of a child awaiting Christmas morning. There was so much to do.

Knock, knock.

CM jerks the door open. "There you are. Come in."

CM doesn't sit behind the desk. Instead, CM takes the seat in front of the desk and indicates that the boss should take the seat behind the desk.

The boss sits down and shares quietly about some of what is happening. He hands CM some notes to read over.

Then, suddenly, the boss stands up and gestures for CM to follow him out of the office. "Bring your notebook." So, CM follows.

Walking through the hallway and on past a main office area, the boss stops various times to talk to others. Winding their way downstairs to the preschool area, the boss pauses to consider one or two of the rooms, filled with workers and children, making some observations for CM to note on the paper.

Still going, the boss heads outside. "Oh, I know" CM thinks, "We're headed out to the gorgeous new prayer garden. It's quiet out there." Yes, they do head to the prayer garden. For a moment, they pause, each silently taking in the glory of creation around them, enjoying the silence offered. But then on again, through the garden and into the parking lot. The boss gets into a car and waits on CM to come sit beside him.

"Where are we going?" CM asks.

"You will see," was the only cryptic answer.

They first drove through an old part of town, run down with its homeless population evident, followed by an upscale neighborhood where young mothers were cramming soccer gear, strollers, and gym bags into their Mercedes. Continuing, they finally stopped at the mall.

Again, the boss gestured for CM to bring the notebook. The mall is teaming with families, groups of teenagers, and others from every walk of life. There is a collage of sights, sounds, and smells. Sitting on a bench at the very center of the mall, the boss said, "Sit. Look. Listen. Note what you learn."

"But aren't you going to tell me what I need to know?"

"Yes, but sit, listen, watch, learn."

As they sat on the bench and watched all that was going on around them, occasionally someone approached the boss, or the two of them would have a conversation about something they saw or heard.

Suddenly, CM gets it. Brain full of thoughts and ideas, the notes fill the page.

When you invite God into the creative process, it's a matter of surrendering control to God, allowing God to be behind the desk.

Think about the writers of each of the books of the Bible. Scripture from Genesis to Revelations is God's message to us. The writers, from Moses to John, were only the vessels through whom these messages are communicated. God's will, God's way, and God's glory.

Easier said than done? What does this look like?

GO TO GOD'S WORD.

Spend time in scripture, not just looking at scripture focused on whatever your project is, but spend time regularly in the Word. Pay attention and note what God is saying. Get to know who God is and what His plan is for you and for the world around you.

STAY CONNECTED.

Prayer is essential. Submit before God. "Lord, Your will, not mine." Bring to God your concerns and needs. Talk to God like you would a friend or your boss.

It's a matter of being connected and staying connected. In 1 Thessalonians 5:17 Paul exhorts believers to "*pray continually*" (NIV). And this is what you should do as you are involved in your creative activity—not just pray at the beginning or end, but continually taking it to God.

Conversation involves both talking and listening. So too is prayer. You need to take time to listen to what God is telling you, whether it is through a still small voice or during the cacophony of noise that often surrounds you in children's ministry. Listen, listen!

Remember that God is the creator of all and is the source of your creativity. If you fail to stay connected to your source, your creative well will dry up. When you stay connected to God you keep supplying the well.

OBSERVE.

As Henry Black in *Experiencing God* notes, you should observe where God is at work and see how you can join Him. Look at those who God has placed in and around your church. What are their perceived and real needs? What work is God doing? Is what you're doing creatively in line with what He is doing and, if not, how can you align it?

How do you see how God is at work? Interact with people, rather than staying hold up in an office. Talk and listen to what is happening in their lives. Study and get to know what the needs are of the generations that you minister to.

Observe trends and patterns. Many years ago, while I was in seminary, I was the volunteer preschool and children's coordinator for my church. The church had been without a pastor for 18 months, so when the new pastor came, volunteers during worship service for our nursery were hard to come by. As I prayed one day, God presented me with a number—15. 15? There were 15 preschool classes and 15 adult Bible study classes. Out of this came the Adopt-a-Preschool class program where each adult class adopted one of the preschool classes and was responsible each week to make sure there were volunteers in their adopted class during worship. A pattern provided an opportunity.

See what God is doing in and through other ministries. Get inspired by (not copy) what others are doing.

And yes, go and sit quietly observing God's glorious creation and let the creative juices flow.

EXERCISE PATIENCE.

God doesn't just tell you yes or no to a prayer need or to some project that you have brought to Him. Sometimes there is a "later."

I don't know how often I have come up with what would be considered great, exiting, cool ideas only to talk them over with God and it's not in the plan for now. Maybe later. That's when I take a slip of paper, write down notes, and store it away for later.

LEARN AND TAKE HELP FROM OTHERS.

You do not serve alone and you are not the only one who needs to be creative. Your ministry is made up of many parts with many gifts. They are not there by accident. God provides not just physical resources for the creative work that He has you do, but He also provides the people resources. I know that I cannot cut or sew. That doesn't mean that creative projects I have been involved in have not needed people who could cut or sew or any of the many other things that I am not talented with. God provides.

You need to not only utilize the gifts and talents of others but listen to them. You and I are not the only ones God has gifted with ideas. Just because you are the primary leader over your ministry does not mean that you are the only source of vision. As a flawed human, you have a limited perspective. By listening to others you can open yourself up to, not just a different view of an issue or event, but to see God through the eyes of another. It's possible that you might learn something about yourself and your ministry.

See what God is doing in and through other ministries both around you and around the world. Through social media you can now see what other ministries are doing, not just down the street but in Alaska, Australia, and Asia. Through others you can see how God is at work and how others are participating in His Work.

How do you know if it is from God?

SCRIPTURE

This is simple. Nothing that God calls you to do will contrast with scripture.

One thing that is important to note is, just because God is involved in the planning doesn't mean that everything you do creatively has to always have a spiritual theme to it. Yes, the focus is supposed to be on the Lord and all is to be for His glory, but when His followers show up and are demonstrating the love of God in what they do, God is present. Look at the book of Esther. The name of God is not once mentioned in the book, but God is very obviously present and active.

CONFIRMATION.

God will provide you with confirmation when you are walking in line with His will and His work. And it can come from the strangest places.

In my church during seminary, there was a man who had been in the church for decades. Just on the principle of things, he always voted no on any issue brought before the church. Therefore, in the time that he had been in the church there had never been a unanimous vote on anything. He was the teacher in the senior adult class and one of the leading deacons. My Adopt-a-Preschool class proposal not only required support of the deacons but would also rely on the participation of all the adult Bible studies. Yes, I confess, I worried about this. Not only did I find out that this man took the lead in persuading the other deacons to support the idea, but he also wanted to go ahead and pick the preschool class that his Sunday school would adopt. This man, who had never served in the nursery in his life, would one time a month bring overalls to put on over his suit and get down on the floor to play with the 2-year-olds and read Bible stories with them. God provided confirmation in a way that only God can.

Keep your eyes, ears, and heart open to all the many ways that God is providing confirmation of what you are doing.

RESULTS.

Am I talking about numbers? Yes and no. Through your failures and successes, you can tell what is in line with God's work. You can see God at work. But sometimes what you see as a failure is not a failure. That one person who read your blog last week? It led them to heal the relationship with their mother. Or the event where only three families showed up? Those three families are now bonding and developing a small group Bible study. Or that amazing lesson you were praised for but that left you feeling flat because God was not a part of it?

Inviting God into your creativity involves taking yourself out of it. Be willing to be the clay for the potter, a vessel to be used for the furtherance of the kingdom. Follow wherever God leads and take notes.

_____

Having been handed her first teacher's book at age 13 and sent in with a class of 2-year-olds, **Ellen Haley** still continues in children's ministry well over 30 years later. A graduate of Southwestern Baptist Seminary in Fort Worth, Ellen has served in full, part-time, and volunteer ministry. She lives in Georgetown, TX and is the founder of FaithFit™Ministry.

chapter 11

LOOK PAST THE TASK LIST
Empowering creatives even when you're not one

BY JOE MALLY

REMEMBER WITH ME FOR A MOMENT. Remember the time when you sat in a meeting or were part of a conversation and ideas were being thrown out, but you just kept drawing a blank. Those around you were running full pace sharing ideas that were good and some that were revolutionary. Yet, you just sat there ... crickets. No one likes this moment. No one likes this moment, because we want to contribute. No one likes this moment, because, try as you might, there is nothing you can do to avoid it completely. As a leader, you often have that feeling that you should always be ready to come up with great new ideas. That's why you can remember that moment well—that moment when you felt like you failed.

There is a tendency to feel as if you must excel in every area of a ministry. In reality, that's not only impossible, but a misunderstanding of the church body. Paul talks about the importance of the church body by saying; *"If the whole body were an eye, where would be the sense of hearing? If the whole body were an ear, where would be the sense of smell? But as it is, God arranged the members in the body, each one of them, as he chose"* (1 Corinthians 12:17-18, ESV). God has equipped every one of us differently and you need to constantly remind yourself of that. It can become a pride issue to want to be good at everything, but it can also inhibit others from doing what God has chosen for them.

How then are you meant to operate? As a believer, you are called to support and work with the other members of the body. You should model this to those around you. You should highlight the members of the body that are gifted in ways you are not. This is not always an easy task to accomplish. When it comes to working with people, there is almost never a one-size-fits-all model. The goal of this chapter, though, is to give you some tools to empower the creative people in your ministry.

It is also important to remember that there are multiple instances where you are gifted in an area and others are not. Finding a balance between these, and a respect for the different giftings we all have, is a task that you must take seriously. Caring for a specific part of the body means caring for the whole body equally. This does not mean treating everyone the same, but it is important to care for everyone. For me, creatives can be the hardest and yet most rewarding people to learn how to work with.

One thing that helped me learn how to work well with creatives was to partner with them on a specific project. Serve alongside them, see how they lead, and recognize how you can serve them. Through this time, you will create camaraderie that will lead to better collaboration in the future. After all, it's important to remember that neither of your personality types is the problem. Instead, focus on establishing trust with each other and allow everyone to lead from their strengths. This trust will form a relationship that will allow both of you to lead well in the years to come.

After you have recognized your own area of gifting, it's time to recruit others to be part of your team. In this recruitment, it is important to make specific strategic asks to allow people to lead not only from their strengths but from areas that give them energy. As you create structure and team flow, consider a system of checks and balances over roles and responsibilities. Let the team be freer in definition and specific in its vision. This will encourage collaboration and allow for the workload to be shared evenly throughout the season. It is important to remember that there is no magic number of members for a creative team when starting out. In my experience, sometimes you start with as little as two and other times it has been ten people. In both of these instances, or when you are working with creatives in general, the principles explained in the rest of this chapter need to be introduced to help you be a good leader or coworker. With this in mind, ask people to join your team and ask them who else should be on the team.

Now that you have recruited a team, you need to clear off the proverbial workbench. Creativity flourishes when it's in the clouds. Chances are as a leader you have multiple items being worked on at one time. Introducing anyone to all of the projects at once could quickly become cumbersome or create a sense of urgency that will stifle creativity. Creatives can multitask well, but start them with a clean slate. Let their inspiration and energy fill the shelves. Creativity will lead to excellence, messiness, and things you would never have started. Yet, these things will lead your ministry to a level beyond where you could take it alone. That's why, before you begin to meet and build the creative team God has placed in your church body, you must first clear out the shop.

Next, you must protect the space given to your creatives. Most of you will not have a physical space designated just for those who lead out creatively in your ministry, but that does not remove the importance of the space when you meet. Creativity flourishes in groups and the space you have for these groups to meet in will encourage or diminish creativity. When choosing a place to meet consider lighting, seating, and noise, but most importantly provide resources to engage in the conversation. Being able to draw, write, and visualize not only will help creatives, but it equips them to communicate better.

Protecting space is not merely about physical space. At some point, your circumstances will demand quick results. In these moments, you will be tempted to exert pressure on the team to produce and create quickly. You must avoid doing this. It's more important to protect your team. It's okay to sacrifice the level of presentation and do it yourself to maintain the integrity of the team. Creativity takes time and space to happen well. While your last-minute project or emergency might seem important in the long run, it is not worth sacrificing the space you have given your team to flourish. It is important to avoid taking on projects from outside of the original vision you casted. Once I broke both of these rules to help make t-shirts for my church in a hurry. My team was rushed to turn them around and did not get why they were being asked to make them. Worse yet, the design they submitted was rejected and they had to start over. This was my failure, not the team's. It took time to rebuild trust that our purpose was to champion the vision and not create products.

Now that the workshop is clear and space is protected, you need to meet as a team around a specific vision. When it comes to creativity, people are your great resource for ideas, collaboration, and success. Cast a vision to those around you and then let them run with it. Pour time into the relationships within this team. Seek individuals who will get along and support one another. A true creative team grows through friendships formed while investing together. Go out of your way to show value and care for their well-being.

Empower them to make decisions and to run at the pace they choose. This empowerment becomes their biggest advocate and cheerleader. Avoid creating systems of recognition; instead, be spontaneous in how you reward or recognize them. Fight battles for them in advance, allowing them not to get weighed down in the politics of it all. One situation I have seen numerous times is the finance conversation. One team I was a part of did not have its own budget which meant every idea, expense, and thought came with a burden of an ask attached to it. Time after time, ideas were thrown out simply because people were tired of asking. Since then, I've always been determined to step into that for them. I've given them the freedom to try and to spend their budget as they choose, instead of making them clear it with me or anyone else.

Earlier, I referenced that creatives like to think in the clouds. My rationale behind this statement is not to say that they can't focus on one thing or never follow through on a project. When I talk about creatives thinking in the clouds, it's to reference the size and scope of how creatives consider a project. If you ask a team to run a VBS for you and then let them go, things will fall through the cracks. However, if you ask a creative team to think through and design the VBS, the scope of the project will be taken into account. Elements, decorations, t-shirts, and everything they touch will be considered in light of the theme that they choose. Why? Because creatives understand the importance of flow and the beauty found in tying things together. They look past the item on the checklist and look at the project as a whole. While this can be frustrating for more task-oriented people, it is a quality to be envied.

With this in mind, it's important to avoid a task list agenda when meeting with individuals. Instead, create clouds representing the project and its scope, but let them interpret it. While you might put choosing a name for something at the top of your list in importance, they will look and see that before you choose a name, x, y, and z need to be chosen. These elements will help inform them and give them guidance for choosing a name that allows them to tie into more elements and bring the project as a whole up in production level.

As production levels rise, remember to celebrate. Give credit where credit is due and recognize individuals' time and talents. As you do that, though, be intentional to identify how that individual or group effort helped to accomplish the vision that you were aiming for. Build into the individual's talents through recognition of how their efforts furthered the team. Be intentional about doing this in failure, too. Recognize how an idea built into the vision of the team and the time spent on it. Avoid criticizing any part of a project but highlight what went well and empower team members to always be trying. The best ideas are not already being used and need to be found. No, the best ideas are found through trial and error and through those errors is when leaders must lead well. Leading well through failure means caring for those involved like you should have all along. However, in that failure is when they will see that you truly are caring for them and protecting them as a leader. If you fail to do so in their failure, all the ground you've gained as a team could be lost as their trust fades away.

Be encouraged, though, because as creatives join your team they are buying into your vision for it. Care for them and they will care for and invest in the ministry in ways you had not thought of. As these things come together, be as hands-off as possible. Offer to be the note taker in the meeting, go get everyone coffee or tea, or just leave for a bit. Make yourself available to clarify or provide guidance but avoid giving suggestions. Let their minds lead them to dream. While they dream together, encourage and support them. Empower them to take risks or to pioneer new territory. Remember your place in the meeting as a leader is to keep them free of other projects, protect their space, empower them to fail, invest in them as individuals, and let them think in the clouds. By doing these things you will create a ministry that empowers creatives to serve and not just be used for their ideas.

Joe Mally is a Christ follower, husband, children's pastor, and coffee addict in that order. His goal in ministry is to partner with churches and families to lead kids to know Christ and grow in their relationship with Him.

chapter 12

ARTICHOKES, DUCT TAPE WARS, AND SPECIAL EVENTS

For the sake of creativity vs. adding value

BY JULIE DEARYAN

THE MYSTERY DINNER INCLUDED artichokes, parsnips, and rambutans (a fruit covered in a prickly skin). My husband had been newly installed as the pastor and since there were no children in the church except our two, we worked together on ideas for special events that would attract families to our church. Displayed was a platter of unusual vegetables and fruits with slips of paper for the kids to guess what vegetable promoted the dinner. Everyone seemed excited about it. The problem was, I had never run a mystery dinner and I was mainly relying on another person's advice about how to do it. The guidance was helpful, but it failed to take into consideration the actual difficulties in running what turned out to be a huge event.

Our Mystery Dinner menu had Bible verses on it that gave cryptic clues for the food the person would order. The Numbers 7:6 Special had the verse, *"And Moses took the wagons and the oxen, and gave them unto the Levites."* This meant if they ordered the Numbers 7:6 Special, they got only a hamburger (oxen). To get a bun, they would need to order from a verse that had the word "bread" in it. If this sounds confusing as you read it, imagine how perplexing it was during the event. We brought out only a hamburger on a plate to one person while another person only received a bun. Then the two of them knew to order the other item so each could have a hamburger with a bun for lunch. This went on for chicken sandwiches, sloppy joes, side dishes, and desserts. I've looked back on that event as one when creativity was used for its own sake rather than adding actual value.

Sometimes, our best ideas can flop. In other cases, our worst ideas can be a huge success. What's the difference? Experience is one. If you've done enough events for your kids' ministry, then you'll start to realize that not all ideas work with the size or the kind of group you have. All ideas must glorify the Lord and bring kids to know and understand the Savior's love. Some ideas facilitate that goal well while others won't.

For years at Christmastime, I worked hard on getting the kids to learn some songs and perform drama for the local community. While these types of events were well received, we couldn't conjure up the kind of talent from our small church to have something that had very good quality. The extra music practices and filming took a toll on our families. When I first broached the idea of doing something more interactive around Christmastime, there were many leaders who loved the idea. Others said they would miss doing our musical. I suggested we try it for one year and then see if the idea worked. If it didn't, I was happy to go back to doing what we'd done before. I had learned about this event from our Kidmin Facebook group. It was called the Christmas Experience. Families signed up ahead to make mangers, gingerbread houses, and contribute to a Christmas cookie contest. We added in a story time with Mary event during the evening, so kids and parents could hear about the real meaning of Christmas.

As we prepared, I was surprised by how easy it was to plan. The set-up was minimal as several men from the church worked together to build wood manger kits for the families to build. We decorated for Christmas which we would've done anyway and made sure to have Christmas music in the parking lot to contribute to the overall experience. I held my breath as the time approached. Would it work? Would families in the community come out and discover the true meaning of Christmas?

CREATIVITY + GOAL = SUCCESS

Our Creator didn't just make one type of flower or one animal. He loves beauty and gave us our ability to be creative. Creativity is more than just thinking of ideas. It is implementing concepts. It is making ideas reality. The reality needs to add value to what you are doing. Some people are so full of ideas that they think every single idea they have must be implemented. The problem is, they often don't understand: how to get the idea to happen or if the notion will add value to the ministry.

Creative thinking means that first you think about the goal you desire. Do you want to reach out into the community? How will new people be the most comfortable coming into the church? Do you want kids and families in your church to grow in the Lord? How can you have events that facilitate growth and learning in the Scripture? When you are creative with these end goals in mind, you'll think more strategically about how to accomplish what you desire. When you combine brainstorming to promote your bottom line goal, then the ideas you come up with will be more strategic.

Successful events need to be creative-oriented, action-oriented, and goal-oriented. Those three things form a symbiotic relationship during the creative process.

When you have events, try not to let yourself get so busy doing them that you lose the ability to observe. Is there excitement and enthusiasm on the part of the kids as they participate? If there isn't, your mind needs to be a little more creative. Listen to what the kids talk about, talk to them about things they're doing, and think about how you can incorporate their ideas into your outreach.

After events, take some time to talk to your volunteers. What did they like most about what happened? What did they like least? What problems can we fix for next time? How could you simplify this event but still have fun? What are some things you heard the kids and families talk about as they participated in this event? When you ask questions, you will learn wonderful tricks and tips about how to make your next event not just another event but a chance to grow together in the Lord. If people aren't giving you insights, consider reframing the question. The book, *Cracking Creativity: The Secrets of Creative Genius,* explains how Toyota asked their workers how they could become more productive. Not many ideas came from this question. When the question was changed to, "How can we make your job easier?" the employees gave great insights and ideas.

Look at events your church is already doing and think about ways you can reinvent it to be more creative and more in tune with what the kids are already doing. Instead of a Harvest Party, have a S.T.E.M. Party with different stations celebrating Science, Math, and so on. Have a biblical application for each one and a devo time at the end to give the Gospel. Or give the Gospel in one of the modules.

Old-fashioned is an easy trend to embrace. Many areas are becoming intrigued with farming, bread baking, gardening, knitting, and wood working. What's old is new again. Invite people who have these skills in your church to demonstrate them for your kids and then have the kids and families work together on a project. It's a way to reach the entire family.

Reject ideas that don't add value to your ministry or aren't easy to do in a group. Things that involve the kids going off campus to do something can be difficult these days. Instead, consider bringing things like petting zoos to your church so that kids can enjoy them, and they don't require you to do a lot to make it a great event.

Have events that challenge a kid's creativity and help them use their God-given abilities. Here are some ideas I've tried. Next to them, I listed a short evaluation of whether the idea worked for me. This doesn't mean that if it didn't happen well for me, it won't work for you! But, hopefully, this will get your creative juices flowing about ways you can innovate with some of the pros and cons of the actual implementation.

EVENT IDEA	DID IT WORK?
Bible Heroes	Kids were supposed to dress as Bible heroes. We have a lot of kids and families that are newly saved so a lot of them didn't really know what Bible heroes even were. This event didn't work that well. Maybe now that we have more kids who know the Bible, it might work better.
Starbucks Café	Worked great. I had hot chocolate with fixings for one of the drinks and a decaf caramel frappaccino that I served in small cups along with some little baked treats. I had it decorated like a real coffee shop. Everyone loved this.

Give Your Leader the Measles	Kids got to put a dot on the leader's face every time they memorized a verse. The kids loved it. The only funny thing was we had a measles outbreak among the Amish during that time and the CDC was out immunizing everyone for the real "measles." Only in kids' ministry, right?
Pirate Princess Walk the Plank	Worked great. Kids loved dressing up as pirates or princesses or a combination of both. If they memorized verses and participated in the evening, they got points. They walked a "plank" (a sturdy table) and when they got to the end, used a fishing pole made from a pool noodle to catch a fish which had a number that correlated to a prize. It was a winning event. I've repeated it several times.
Geo-Caching Scavenger Hunt	We divided the teens into groups with a driver for each vehicle. They had coordinates they programed into a maps app on a phone to find previously hidden objects. This was a winning event and generated a lot of excitement since real geo-caching had become popular. This worked for us because at the time, we were a smaller group. I think with a bigger group, it would be harder to implement.
Donut Stacking	The kids had a blast with this but the cleanup was not fun. It would've been better if we could've done this event outside. I just bought a bunch of day-old donuts (tried to only have plain) and the kids stacked them in games and made structures out of them. The Bible lesson was "Donut Quit"—how God will never stop loving us.

Glow in the Dark and Warm Chocolate Chip Cookies	This was a wonderful event and relatively easy. Any superstore has tons of items and games that are glow in the dark. I turned out just enough of the lights to make it fun and the warm chocolate chip cookies made it special. This is an example of how a simple idea can be turned up a notch into something even more fun. If I had served chocolate chip cookies, it would have been a good event. But baking them right before we served them, made the evening more fun without a lot of extra work.
Duct Tape Wars	A great event and fun for all ages. We brought in some huge boxes from a company that donated them. We also had a ton of boxes that people brought. When everyone got there, we divided into teams, gave them rolls of duct tape and had them get to work making shields, swords, and structures out of the cardboard and duct tape. At the end of a designated time, they got to try to destroy each other's structures with their cardboard swords. The structure that held up the best was the winner. This is a good event for many ages to do together. The lesson was about how the wise man builds his house on God's foundation so it can't be destroyed.
Food Around the World	I've had this type of event several times and it's always easy and successful. A visit to almost any grocery store has snack foods from different places. I put out the foods along with a sign saying where the food is from. I try to get foods from where our missionaries are located and our Bible teacher uses that time to share about our missionaries.

Decorate Your Own Superhero Cape	This was a fun event. I had everyone bring old t-shirts that they cut off the arms and the front leaving the neck. This formed a cape. They decorated them with fabric paint, iron on letters, etc. The Bible lesson was how Jesus is our superhero coming to do for us what we couldn't' do for ourselves by dying on the cross for our sins.
Slimed	This event evokes mixed feelings from me. I loved it but it was very messy and ultimately I'm not sure it was worth it. We played a bunch of games outside with slime we created and also each of the kids got to take some home. At the end, we slimed my husband who is the pastor of the church. I feel bad about this, because I was trying to come up with something green looking to slime him with and added some hot banana pepper juice to the mixture. I don't know what I was thinking because when the "slime" went down his face, it burned his skin. Not one of my better ideas. The Bible lesson on this was how we are messy spiritually and only God can clean us up.
Root Beer / Creamsicle Floats	Worked great! Easy too.

By the way, the Christmas Experience turned out wonderfully. I got to circulate around the different areas talking to brand new families. I felt relaxed (which I have never felt during our musicals) and enjoyed the entire evening. Over 100 people heard the Gospel during our story time with Mary. The entire event was a resounding success that other people wanted to do again. Doing Christmas differently showed me that creativity is important but also almost as equally vital is getting people on board and working together to create something that contributes to the goal of reaching people with the Gospel. Make sure your creativity contributes value to the vision.

Julie Dearyan is a kidmin leader in a country church. She enjoys hanging out with her twin granddaughters and coming up with creative ideas to bring families to know more about the Lord.

chapter 13

DON'T RELY ON THE AUDIBLE

A strong game plan wins championships

BY STACY MARKS

I ENJOY WATCHING SPORTS. Let's be honest, some sports are much more exciting to watch from my living room than others. Football is often my living room sport of choice. Grab some nachos and hot wings, invite some friends over, sit back and enjoy. And sometimes, it happens—the quarterback calls an audible. At the edge of our seats we watch the game winning throw, the Hail Mary pass, the run into the in-zone, the dive to the touchdown. It's the creative moment that makes the game memorable.

Sometimes, I wish every game had that exciting finish. I wish life could be run on the audible. But the fact is, winning championships, in any game, takes a strong play book. A plan—a well-executed plan—by a team and a coach who are in it together, wins championships. The audible play, which is creative by nature, is most effective because of a solid foundation.

I have often thought that creativity is spur-of-the-moment. It's a moment of greatness that I stumble upon. It's the audible that takes us to another level of ministry, makes our program more effective, makes our rooms more inviting, and makes our message more memorable. Those audible plays usually happen when I get in the shower, or at 2 am before an event. But the truth is, these audible plays cannot be where creativity lives in our ministry. Creativity needs to be fostered, scheduled, and planned in our "long-term playbook" so that we can be creativity champions.

SCHEDULING

Let's be honest, scheduling and calendaring should probably be considered a spiritual gift. You, as a ministry leader, either love it or hate it. Scheduling often seems to be the opposite of creativity. But to bring your creativity to the next level, a well thought out schedule is the foundation of your playbook.

There is no perfect way to schedule your year and your ministry. God has perfectly placed you in your position. Talk to Him and find your rhythm. In our ministry, we do long-term planning for the next calendar year the September of the year before. This is all-church planning, and every department is tasked with placing big events on the calendar, turning in budgets, and making the next year one that is glorifying to God, with the goal of reaching our city, county, and the world for the Lord.

Because of my September due date, my team and I begin dreaming about the new year in the summer. It used to be a lunch date, a team meeting, and more recently a camping trip, to dream about the future. We look at the curriculum schedule and decide what big concepts we are teaching. We put big events on the calendar. The foundation is complete ... and then, the magic happens.

The game plan or schedule tells you where each week or each month, each event or each series is taking you, and now it's time to dream! You have now made time to add creative elements to your program. Friends, this doesn't happen naturally for all of us. A dreaming session might also need to be calendared for you and your team. But I've found that because you know where you're going, and your play book is all set, you can then answer questions that foster creativity. After the foundation is placed, you know where you're going and when. The next step is to answer the HOW. How will you creatively communicate the Gospel to children? How will it look? How will kids enter the room? How will you communicate with families? Dream, and dream big!

REVIEW AND REPLAY

Football players watch game films, and they do it over and over and over. In our hometown, a mom posted a picture of eight 10-year-old players at a pizza place, before a championship game, watching films of past games. The coaches were reviewing plays, refining their playbook, and studying the other team's past games. They were prepared for the championship. The same thing should be happening in your ministry.

Are you giving yourself and your team time for review? Is it on your calendar? My boss, and senior pastor, Eric Daniel, often says in staff meeting, "If it doesn't get written down, it doesn't get done!" (He may have stolen this quote from someone else, but today he gets the credit!) You know you should review an event, but you forget to schedule the meeting, or just do it in passing. How often are you reviewing your events, midweek program, Sunday program, children's church, or Sunday school programs?

We have a Sunday evening service at Hillside at 6:30 pm. My staff comes at 5:30 pm for pre-service prayer, which is over by 6:00 pm. By 6:05 pm we are always in the rocking chairs of the nursery, not just to chat and laugh (although let's be honest a lot of laughter happens in ministry). We know that we have 10-15 minutes to do a quick review of our morning programming.

We can download the good, the bad, and the ugly of Sunday morning, so that we can quickly solve any programming issues on Sunday night. We also can make a To-Do list for the next week of areas that need strength, prayer, or to be celebrated.

This is not my team's only time of review. We have scheduled meetings (usually at my favorite Mediterranean restaurant) to go over what was amazing, and what needs to be re-tooled. How can we do it better? Where do we need to add a creative element to be more effective? What worked? What didn't? Where are we going next? We "go over the films" of events and programs. We know what we did well and where we can improve. Reviewing, and reviewing often, allows you to push to new levels of creativity, because you're always trying to do it better.

EVERYTHING ON THE TABLE

This year I've been at Hillside Christian Church in Napa, CA for a decade. Ten full years of ministry in one location (and in my hometown no less) is a huge accomplishment. I just promoted a group of 5th graders to youth ministry. Many of them were in the nursery when I came on staff at Hillside.

My ministry at Hillside has grown. People like it. It has a good reputation. It has its challenges and weaknesses, and I am aware of them, but we're doing a good job, for the most part. But this year, after a decade of ministry, I put everything on the table. Good ministry doesn't rely on an old playbook. It can't. The culture is changing, kids are changing, our community is changing. The truth of God's Word? That never changes (and aren't we thankful), but how we creatively communicate that truth must always continue to be relevant. So, this year, in our planning, I put everything on the table. Essentially, I looked at my assistant and said, "We're throwing out the old playbook, because the Lord has more for us, and for the kids of Napa."

I don't have time for business as usual if I want kids and their families to hear the Gospel message. The events we had been doing were creative and fun and memorable, but it was time to give room for the Holy Spirit to stir up something new in our ministry and in my heart. This, my friends, was a scary moment. Everything I had done so well, my whole playbook from the last decade was laid open, ready to be rewritten, rescheduled, and retooled. But ... it was awesome!

Today, because we gave time to schedule and plan, we're looking at the fall with new eyes and a fresh vision. I told my husband last week, "In the fall, children's ministry is going to look a whole lot different. It's going to be unrecognizable." I am so excited. The Lord is going to unearth something new in me and is taking me and my team to new levels of creativity. Not so we have the best looking ministry in town, but so kids and their families can hear the Gospel message in new ways—so we can be more effective communicators of the Gospel of Jesus.

PLAYING THE AUDIBLE

Sometimes playing the audible is the only way to win the game. A team that is scheduled, practiced, and strong, can be flexible, change the plan, and win the championship.

When your schedules are strong, you know where you're going, you have things ordered in advance, and teams are prepped and ready, then you can play an audible to win. Sometimes creativity hits you when you least expect it. I've been up in the middle of the night with one of my boys and come up with a new idea for a lesson or series we're about to teach. Just last week, as I was teaching our preschool large group lesson, the Lord downloaded to me a vision of a new preschool event that would enhance our fall program and goals. It's so exciting when the Lord gives you new dreams, visions, and ideas of what your ministry could be and how it could impact your community.

When a schedule and plan is strong, you can easily call an audible. Because I am not frantically shopping for supplies the day before my event, I can easily run to the store to grab something for an object lesson I've just come up with. Because we have a schedule of our fall curriculum planned and ready to go, my mind can dream bigger and do more in our preschool department in the fall. A solid plan allows my team to be more creative and do ministry with excellence. Because my team knows where we're going, we have the space to do more, make our ministry a more creative and better experience, and be more effective in our community.

GATHER THE BEST TEAM

One of the very best things about thinking ahead, for more creative ministry, is that it allows me to bring others along with me. Running the "Stacy Marks" show is never my goal in ministry. To grow a church, to grow a ministry, and to do it creatively, it takes a team. Some of our best ideas have happened when my leadership team comes together and goes over the playbook. Now, to be fair, if everyone is calling plays from the sidelines, and no one knows who the coach is, the whole game will be utter chaos. But, when you know your position on the team, and give ideas and suggestions based on your position, your team will be better because of it.

If you are the head coach, like I am in my ministry, you should be coming to a planning and creative meeting with an overarching vision and plan that you can communicate well. You should be spending time with the Lord and have clarity from Him and a clear vision for your ministry (Note: Make sure to talk to your senior leaders about your plans and visions. All your vision and plans should align with the entire church.) If you are a ministry leader, maybe you could be called the offensive coordinator or the defensive line coach. Maybe you take on the role of the "kicker." Whatever your title is, whatever your position on the team, you can add to the creativity and effectiveness of your ministry! Every position on the team can push the team to greater creativity, planning, and effectiveness. Iron sharpens iron, right?

DON'T RELY ON THE AUDIBLE

When I know my "game plan" well in advance, it also gives me an opportunity to invite the creativity of others. When I, as the "head coach," knew that we were going to do our Vacation Bible School as a Super Hero theme, I gathered a team of experts around me. Because I wanted to make that event as creative as possible, I worked on all the spiritual concepts, and then gathered around me a team of ... well ... "super hero nerds" for lack of a better term. (It's an endearing term really, as one of them was my sweet husband.) They added their creativity and expertise to our event. In the fall we're doing a camping theme and telling each of our stories as campfire stories, so I've gathered a team of great teachers and storytellers (and a few avid glampers like myself) to come alongside me to write our new curriculum. Because our schedule is well planned, I can invite the right players to join with me.

WIN THE CHAMPIONSHIP

The key to a strong playbook in kids' ministry doesn't just rely on scheduling, coordination, and creativity. The Holy Spirit is your Most Valuable Player, to keep with my football analogy, and must be called upon. The goal is not just creativity, although creative methods are vital. The goal is to help introduce people to Jesus. Keep that in mind, as you push your ministry forward and allow the Holy Spirit to lead and guide your team to victory!

Stacy Bingham Marks is a proud "boymom" (even the dog and the fish are boys), Disneyland expert, glamping enthusiast, law enforcement wife, and children's pastor. For the past 10 years, she has been blessed to be part of Hillside Christian Church in Napa, CA.

117

chapter 14

RUT TO GROOVE

Group brainstorming hacks

BY KAL OTIS

"You cannot mandate productivity; you must provide the tools to let people become their best." - Steve Jobs

A CLUSTER OF IDEAS, with team creativity and collaboration, has the power to give birth to the greatest idea ever! You may think you aren't creative, but think again! This great myth will sabotage you into not leading a brainstorming session with your teams. The God of this universe has uniquely handcrafted you in His image. *"God created man in His image"* (Genesis 1:27, ESV). We're not creative because of our talents. We're creative because that's how God made us. It's God's image in us that gives us the capacity to use our imaginations to do something good, find unique solutions, solve problems, and help others.

I've found when we believe a myth, it has the power to control and limit our God-given potential. The myth becomes a reality. Take Matt for instance. He was part of a remarkable team and had tremendous potential. But Matt had convinced himself he wasn't creative. He sat quietly in our first brainstorming meeting, nervous, that if he spoke up, someone would think it was a silly idea. He was a computer genius who solved complex computer problems with unusual ease. No doubt he was creative, but the myth had influenced him to believe that he wasn't creative, just "nerdy."

Many of us were taught to "stay inside the lines" and to "cut a pattern exactly as instructed." This teaches you to think safely. But creativity calls you to explore and dabble with the unsafe, uninhibited, risky, what-if thinking. It moves you from rut to groove. Groove implies movement ... and with style. It's exhilarating to lead a team in a creative brainstorming session where imaginations ignite, barriers are overcome, and an idea gains traction.

Check out the following concepts to get your mind primed and ready as the facilitator. These are building block principles that can be used to encourage your team to think differently so they can contribute their best to the group's brainstorming process. It's worth noting that there's no beginning or end; this implies that all of these concepts work together to maximize team creative thought.

Brainstorming is simply the process of crafting new ideas and solutions through collective imaginative thinking to create a new groove. Consider the following before you invite others into the brainstorming process.

WHY SHOULD WE DO THIS?

Let's explore some of the reasons.

- In order to advance the Kingdom, change is essential to reach the lost. The reality is that we can't solve this year's problems with last year's solutions. Brainstorming is a mentally challenging way to ditch the rut and generate new ideas. The process will rally a team that understands and champions change.

- Creative brainstorming triggers personal growth and provides impetus to dream, be inspired, and take action. It stretches your thinking and gets you out of a rut. It gives you the space to look at a problem from a different perspective.

- As the leader you need this fun and creative time with your teams. This is a perfect opportunity to get crazy, dream big, play with ideas, be illogical and impractical, without sweating over the decision-making and details! How many meetings have you attended where you walk out wanting your two hours back? Well, if you set the stage correctly, everyone will walk away encouraged and motivated about the future.

- Additionally, your team will have fun with each other. They will get to know their teammates better and learn to be a unified team. It gives team members a safe platform to voice their ideas, which provides personal validation and encouragement. It makes them an integral part of future vision development.

- Problem solving. I'm not talking about team conflict, but those that arise due to old or non-efficient systems. For example, you might come to the conclusion you're stuck in an ineffective rut in how you track attendance or do social media. You can bring this to your team and brainstorm together to generate a list of innovative solutions. Team-thought will produce more options than individual ideating.

- Team brainstorming allows you to get a pulse on each team member's strengths and weaknesses. You will discover that some naturally generate ideas while others are great at making those ideas workable. Some live to discover resources, and others are doers who love to execute. The key is to recognize each person's natural ability, encourage it, and spur them on to growth.

- I recognize that most teams are heavy with logical and practical thinkers. Not everyone is comfortable thinking outside the context of what's normally acceptable. This is why I'm focusing on the brainstorming session, the process, and its benefits. There will be time for practical thinking later, so maximize this time to dream!

ENVIRONMENT

- An environment can either stimulate and jump-start the brain or cause it to go into funk mode. Stay away from boring, as well as default, meeting rooms. This sets your team up to feel zero team synergy. Try different venues. I've tried coffee shops, pizza places, a home of a team member, a camping lodge, a very large room with lots of space, a garden, picnic tables outside on a beautiful day ... you get the idea. See what inspires you and gives the team energy. I've taken my teams to the mall as well as the grocery store to simply people watch. I wanted them to ask the Lord to give them a renewed passion for lost souls. The brainstorming session that followed was very productive.

- Consider an environment that is appealing to the senses. Look for rooms that are colorful, smell pleasant, and have comfortable seating. Regulate temperature so it's not too warm or too cold. Bring appropriate props as well as use apps such as Moodstream or Visual Thesaurus to enhance associative thinking.

- Mix it up a little. Create real-life experiences that transport your team to think differently. I once asked my team to exit and reenter our building as guests. I gave them different names and paired a few up to be a family. They saw things in a completely different light. Instead of becoming defensive about established guest systems, they were able to own the fact that we need to update what we were doing to improve first-time guest experience.

- Seat everyone in a circle. This creates a safe neutral space, with a focus that moves from person to person. It's a welcoming arrangement where everyone is seen and heard. It invites participation even from Silent Sally.

- Food intake sparks creative thought processes. It's just another way to make the session fun, refreshing, and relaxing. Surprise your team by serving their favorite snacks and drinks. If you're working on a thematic project, provide themed snacks.

Use tools to record and visualize the progress of ideas. This allows the team to see the flow of ideas and give them context around next steps. Search the web for mind mapping as well as team collaboration apps that allow you to build, save, generate, and share ideas with your team. Experiment with free trial apps to determine the best fit. Popplet is my team's favorite app. Easels, giant sticky notepads, and several colored permanent markers are a must, if apps are not your preferred tool. I like using both. I've had better experiences with giant sticky notepads rather than whiteboards, because it helps the team visualize everything as well as gives them a feeling of accomplishment when the papers are hung all over the room!

UNDERSTANDING THE PROCESS

Room to Think. Gather everyone in the room, present a problem or a project, and then give them time to brainstorm away from the crowd. Give your team members time to think through and jot down their ideas independently before jumping into the next phase. I encourage my team to do whatever they want to do to spark their imaginations. Some wander away, go for a walk, stare into space, go to their offices, cruise the internet, listen to music, pace ... it's fun to watch! This allows ideas to flow freely without any influence and intimidation. After they all return, we go to the defer judgment phase.

Defer Judgment Phase. A healthy brainstorming session will defer judgment and give freedom to create and generate new ideas, no matter how hare-brained, far-fetched, or completely over budget they are! These moments are for dreaming, exploring, building on ideas, creating connections between ideas, breaking your own rules, and daring to risk failure. It's a time to focus on quantity over quality of ideas. There's no room to be negative or critical, formulate a plan, think about money, embrace fear, cling to reality, be logical, or think of all the reasons why it can't work. That's for another time. The total focus needs to be on creative thinking only. If planning and execution comes into play too early, all of your creative power will diminish. You, as the team leader, must guard this process vigorously!

Usually, I spend a lot of time on open brainstorming before I proceed to the practical phase. You might devote an entire morning to brainstorming and then move to the next phase in the afternoon. When you feel that you've exhausted your options and have discovered some great ideas through the process, then (and only then) move on to the next phase.

The Practical Phase. This is where you visualize all the ideas and, through discussion, narrow them down to the best options. This is when you put on your practical question hat and think about how you can implement these ideas. Expense, time, feasibility, and the like are considered. After you've narrowed the list down to a set of best ideas, you move to the execution phase.

Execution Phase. This last phase is where you, as a team, pound out the details of how you will make this idea come to life. Set goals, deadlines, budget, manpower, and all necessary details to make it happen. Then celebrate and be excited about what you've accomplished together!

Note that it's important to talk to your team about the importance of unity once you've settled on an idea. I can't overemphasize this enough. Make it your goal to make sure everyone is totally committed to the final idea or ideas. Agree together that the Lord has led you to this place and when criticism comes (which it will, if you're thinking creatively), everyone stands united in his or her conviction of giving the idea a try. No gossip. No negative talk. Only trusting God for the outcome!

GUIDELINES AND CLEAR DIRECTIONS FOR BRAINSTORMING

It's very important to give your team specific guidelines and clear directions before you start. If you don't, you may not achieve the desired end result and you will probably run into a brick wall. Here are some suggested guidelines to avoid team frustration.

1. Remember, this is a linear process that must follow a particular order to succeed. Various team members will want to jump right into the details, offer a list of reasons as to why the idea can't possibly work, interrupt, and/or actually put a team member down for their idea. The team needs to have a clear understanding of their leader's set boundaries and the rules of the game before they engage in a brainstorming session.

2. You can't allow put-downs, sarcastic remarks, negative comments, or anything that would hinder the creative process. You must protect your people, especially your more introverted members, like Silent Sally, so they feel safe to contribute more than once. You will encounter long-winded Dominant Donald and Storyteller Stacy who will try to explain every detail of their idea, but don't allow it! Keep this time limited to thoughts, ideas, connections, and "what-ifs" to generate building blocks for more. Distractible Donna can be good at this because it requires "soft thinking" skills, which include random and abstract thinking.

3. Everyone must share at least two ideas. This puts Silent Sally at ease because she knows she will have the chance

to share, while Dominant Donald and Monologue Mike realize that they have limited time. I've found that over time, Silent Sally often earns the respect of the team and the team is eager to hear her ideas.

4. Keep the sessions moving so that everyone has room to create. Avoid the stall out moments by asking more questions and motivating the team to move to the next best idea. Take breaks when you think the team needs a breather or before a new problem or concept is introduced.

5. If possible, include a variety of people with different backgrounds and experiences. Allowing people to be creative includes their story. Although we strive to challenge our thinking, everyone still brings a unique perspective to the group.

6. Start each session with improvisational games or warm-ups. (I live for this!) It allows your team to relax, laugh, and open their minds to what's to come. I have files full of brainstorming warm-ups and team building exercises that are not only fun, but serve a purpose. Don't skip this step! This helps members temporarily forget their stress and relax!

7. After warm-ups, start your brainstorming segment by giving your team parameters, i.e. group key words, concepts, themes, problems, or objects to start with. Give them a starting point or they'll be all over the map. If you are brainstorming about a certain concept, like an event, make your final objective clear and then ask how it can be accomplished. Your starting point can be a final outcome goal, a specific problem, a scriptural concept ... anything you want or need to accomplish.

8. Take pictures and record everything clearly as the session progresses. Give your team immediate access to everything via a shared app or document so they can continue to digest ideas and develop them further.

9. Allow people to add ideas after the session. I'm a proces-
sor and my team knows that some of my best ideas come
long after the session is over.

10. Keep your brainstorming leadership muscles in shape.
Read, listen to podcasts, and rub shoulders with those
who do this well. I've learned a lot by inviting myself to
attend sessions at successful businesses that do this well.

THE SWEET SPOT

As a leader, it's exciting to encourage the next idea, ask questions, inspire your team to create, and watch them get excited. When you facilitate brainstorming meetings, ideas start to gush out of people; allow the process to flow. There is a sweet spot between being a Mr. Doormat and being Mr. Militant! The trick is to facilitate boldly, motivate gently, and inspire energy without slamming the door on the progress prematurely. The more you engage in brainstorming sessions with your teams, the more you will have the opportunity to train yourself to discern when to step in or back off. You will learn to trust your instincts.

As your team frequently dreams and brainstorms together, their new groove will generate some real and viable ideas. The best ideas will surface and take your ministry to the next level for God's namesake. The best part is that when you create spaces for others to use their creativity, not only does the church win, but also the world gets a display of God's character in you.

With 30 years of ministry experience, **Kal Otis** enjoys creating spaces where multi-generational teams can use their individuality, creativity, and unique learning styles to be who God has called them to be. Besides leading the family ministry team at South Park Church she loves when friends and family stop by to raid her fridge and sit at her dining table. blog: kalotis.com

chapter 15

JESUS ISN'T ALWAYS THE ANSWER

*Avoiding Sunday school answers
by asking the right questions*

BY ASHLEY KUHN

THERE IS A COMIC OF A LITTLE BOY in a math class. He steps up to the chalkboard and prepares himself to answer the equation $2 + 2 =$ ___. He says to the teacher, "I'm pretty sure the answer is 4, but my mama says, 'Jesus is always the answer.'" As a children's ministry leader, you ask questions for many reasons. You ask questions to build relationships, to review or clarify what the children think you taught them, to increase empathy and understanding, to engage their senses, to expand their critical thinking, and much more! Questions are important.

All people, being created in the image of God, are given the opportunity to answer questions all the time. It's an integral part of your God-given free will. You get to make decisions based on the questions that come up in your life. What will I wear today? Will I eat the lunch my mom packed? Who will I be friends with? Will I steal that candy? Where will I go to college? What will I be when I grow up? Who will I marry? Will I obey the Lord out of a thankful heart? God gave you the opportunity to come up with your own answers to decisions and questions all around you.

THERE'S NO SUCH THING AS A DUMB QUESTION, BUT THERE ARE BETTER ONES.

There's a common phrase, "There's no such thing as a dumb question." However, I believe, as a kidmin leader you can ask better questions. Asking true or false and multiple-choice questions are good for confirming what children learned, clarifying their head knowledge. However, if you want to assess their heart knowledge and create a space for spiritual growth, you need to ask better questions. For example, after teaching the story of Jesus feeding the 5,000 you can ask, "How many fish and loaves of bread did Jesus start with?" This would elicit a head knowledge response. These kinds of questions definitely have a place in ministry. This allows time to assess if what your kids learned is actually what you taught. Or you could ask, "Why do you think Jesus fed the people instead of sending them away?" The first question is an easy fact question. It tests children to see how well they were paying attention to the details of the story. The second question invites children to dig deeper and ponder the heart of God. See how there can be a better question?

Asking questions that require empathy or feelings helps children grow in their faith by putting themselves in the shoes of the characters you are speaking about. "How do you think the young boy felt when he offered his lunch to the disciples?" You can ask sensory questions to help children imagine what it was like to be there. "What do you think the bread and fish tasted like after Jesus blessed it?" Invoke their imaginations with questions like, "What if you were that boy. Can you imagine giving your lunch to Jesus?" Then take it one step further and ask, "What can you give Jesus?"

Before you ask a question, ask yourself, "What is my intention with this question?" Do I want the children to recite rote facts? Do I want to measure their success/growth? Do I want to increase their empathy? Do I want them to consider making a heart change? Asking these questions will help you determine what kind of questions you should ask to inspire critical thinking.

THERE ARE BETTER ANSWERS, TOO.

Not only is it important to consider the question you ask, but you also need to think about how the children are to respond. Sometimes, in a large group setting, you can't have all 30 kids answer, "What if you were that boy? What lunch would you give Jesus?" You would run out of time, quickly! You need to gear your question to your audience. You could ask this question in a small group or one-on-one, but large groups would be tricky. Imagine, instead, if you asked your large group, "Think about what lunch you would give Jesus. When you have an idea rub your tummy." This inspires all kids to be involved, doesn't take up too much time, and even leaves space for the shy or introverted child to participate.

We have a little boy in our class who is terrified to speak in the large group time. Colby will not answer a question in a large group, because he is far too shy. We used to play review games where a question was asked and each child raced to the front of the room to answer it. Colby purposefully threw the race, intentionally losing, just so he wouldn't have to answer the question. Please, make me a promise right now, don't give up on your Colby. Give him time to warm up to you. Give him opportunities to answer questions, without the whole children's church staring at him. Even if he never raises his hand in class, I can guarantee that he is listening. He is thinking of the answers. He just doesn't want to be embarrassed. Find ways to involve your Colby in critical thinking that won't put him on the spot.

Make sure you always ask questions and receive the child's answer gracefully. One December morning, after discussing all about the wise men coming to visit baby Jesus, a teacher asked, "What were the three gifts the wise men brought?" Sammy confidently shot his hand into the air. The teacher called on him. He proudly stated that the gifts were "Gold, frankincense, and worms!" Now the teacher had a choice. How will she respond? Will she laugh? Will she tell him he is wrong? Will she say, "Two out of three ain't bad"? Before she responds, she needs to think about how Sammy will feel. If she laughs, will Sammy laugh too? Or will he get upset and cry? If she lovingly corrects him, will he accept the correction and move on? Did he give this incorrect answer on purpose to elicit a response from the crowd? Consider how you would gracefully respond to Sammy's incorrect answer.

STEAL IDEAS FROM A LITTLE BLUE DOG.

Give children time to answer. Awkward silences are just that ... awkward. However, when asking questions, sometimes they are necessary. Blue's Clues was a forerunner in the revolution of children's TV shows. They had a team full of researchers well educated in childhood development and psychology. The team, led by Angela Santomero, researched Sesame Street (the leading childhood television show of its time) in the development of Blue's Clues. Blue's Clues is known for its interactive questions that actively involve viewers to follow Steve's dog Blue and her clues, right along with Steve and the gang. Blue, the dog, leaves paw prints on clues to communicate with Steve. Steve and the audience work together to figure out what these clues mean.

Children learn more from a curriculum, Bible lesson, or even a television show if they are actively involved. Active audience participation encourages ownership. Blue's clues researchers intentionally created the show with active audience participation to encourage mastery of thinking and problem-solving skills. Steve asks a question and strategically pauses to allow time for children to answer. As a children's leader, you have been taught to avoid awkward silences. You try to answer questions for the children if the room gets too quiet. However, children need some time and silence to process questions. Don't rush it! Provide age-appropriate pacing and explicit instructions on how to answer the question you present.

Blue's clues had a mission to fully research each episode and determine if it was up to the standards. They employed consultants on each episode. Angela Santomero has a master's degree in child developmental psychology from Columbia University. This group is definitely well educated and a good resource for children's ministers. The show's call and response format was copied by several shows including Dora the Explorer, Jake and the Neverland Pirates, and Go Diego Go. Sesame Street even decided to reformat their segments to be more interactive after noting the popularity of Blue's Clues. If Sesame Street can steal Blue's philosophy of questions, so can the church! Ask age-appropriate questions and pause to allow time for responses.

"WHAT DID YOU LEARN AT CHURCH TODAY?" "I DON'T KNOW."

Parents and kidmin leaders can use questions to build relationships with their children. However, too many times the adult feels shut-down by one-word or limited responses.

"Did you have a good day?" "Yes."

"How was your lunch?" "Okay."

"Hey mom look at this!" "What is it?" "A cow, duh!"

What if the mom with the cryptic cow drawing asked a question that did not end in a question mark. I know that sounds like an oxymoron, but roll with me here. Instead of asking, "What is it?" she could ask the child to "Tell me about your art!" Ask leading questions to get a response. Instead of, "How was your lunch?" try asking, "What was the tastiest part of your lunch? What part did you throw away?" You need to be creative when asking questions. If you want to get better answers, you need to ask better questions. The purpose of these questions are to create relationships, so ask questions relationally. "Did you have a good day?" could become, "Who did you spend time with today?" "What was your favorite part of the day?" "Tell me something that made you laugh today." "When were you happiest today?" "When were you bored today?" "If you could be the teacher tomorrow, what would you do?" There are so many ways to ask, "How was your day?"

QUESTIONS FROM A GOLDFISH BOWL

Our youth pastor has a special night once a month when he sets a goldfish bowl out and allows the teens to write any question they have and put it in the bowl. On their goldfish bowl night, he attempts to answer these questions. Some of these questions are biblical facts, some are relational, some are hygiene! You never know what kind of questions will come up. You're probably thinking, "Doesn't he worry about being put on the spot like that?" or "What if they ask a question, and he doesn't know the answer?" He is humble enough to say, "I don't know, but I can find out." You can allow time for children to ask questions. Sometimes, they might be tough biblical questions. I had a boy ask me today, "How long (distance) did the Israelites walk in the Red Sea when God separated the waters?" I said, "I don't know, let's google it!" After lots of research, we found that ... we don't really know! Some believe it was as little as 50 meters. Some say it was as much at 18 kilometers. The Red Sea itself has a maximum width of 190 miles, so we know it should be less than that.

JESUS ISN'T ALWAYS THE ANSWER

Honestly, you just don't know which path Moses led the Israelites to use. What's important to know is that God provided
a way for His people. He provided a path to salvation from the
Egyptian army, and more importantly, a path to salvation from
our sins. See how you can take a child's question and use it to
draw so much more out? Allowing children time to ask questions allows the child to feel ownership in the lesson.

ANY QUESTIONS?

Questions are a beautiful thing. Questions can allow you to
review and clarify lessons. Questions can invoke the imagination and engage the senses. Questions can increase empathy.
Questions can expand critical thinking skills. Questions can
create and build relationships. Questions can lead a child to
Christ! Be intentional with the questions you ask, how you ask
them, when you ask them, and how you answer them.

Ashley Kuhn is a proud member of the MOB, Moms Of Boys.
She has 2 little boys ages 6 and 4, and is married to her high
school sweetheart. She's the children's pastor at Shepherd
Church of the Nazarene in Columbus, OH.

chapter 16

YOU'RE HOT!

How to get the right feedback

BY EMILY HILL

A S I WAS DRIVING MY DAUGHTERS (3 & 5 years old) to the babysitter's house one morning, they were chatting with each other in the back seat about all of the outdoor adventures they were going to have that day. At one point, my 5-year-old talked about swimming, playing on the swing set, and coloring with sidewalk chalk. She turned and asked her sister what she would like to do. My precious 3-year-old responded by telling her sister that she wanted to poop in the yard. (I sincerely hope you're not offended by toilet humor, but if you work with kids surely you're used to it by now!) I promise that I'm telling you this heartwarming tale for a reason.

My daughter was genuinely looking for feedback when she was talking with her sister about the activities planned for the day, but she made a couple of errors. She asked the wrong question and the wrong person. (If you've ever interacted with a 3-year-old, you know what I mean.)

Getting the right feedback is all about understanding what you need to know, who to ask, and how to ask. Once you get that figured out you can begin collecting valuable information to further the ministry that God has called you to lead.

HOT AND COLD

If you're a living breathing human being, there are probably multiple times every single day that you desire feedback on something. It could be the meal you prepared for dinner (yay, this was delicious!) or the new shirt you bought (wow, you look great!) It could be the backyard project you completed (this is amazing!) or the spreadsheet you completed at work (this is so helpful, great job!) You thrive on feedback because it helps you gauge if you're going in the right direction.

Do you remember playing the hot/cold game when you were a kid? A child hid an item while the other closed his eyes. Once it was hidden, the child went searching for the hidden item. The child who hid it would assist with verbal cues by saying, "You're cold" when not close to the item at all and respond by saying, "Getting warmer" as they got closer to the hidden item. When they were very close, the child would shout, "You're hot!" and the other child would soon find the item. The verbal temperature indicators aided in finding the hidden item.

Just like in the hot/cold game, there are things in life and ministry that can become hidden from you. Verbal feedback aids let you know how you're doing. Looking at it from a ministry perspective, it could be that you run a large program and it's literally impossible for you to see everything that goes on. It could be that you're so busy meeting with volunteers prior to service that you don't have the opportunity to talk with parents regularly. It could be that you're teaching one class on Sunday mornings while four other classes are going on. It could be that your volunteers talk amongst each other but don't share their concerns with you. It could be so many other possibilities too, depending upon your ministry size and structure.

LET'S EAT

Ministry to children involves interactions with a lot of different people: volunteers, parents, kids, other staff members, everyone else in the church that has an opinion. As a leader in ministry, it's important for you to realize and appreciate the value in obtaining feedback from all of these sources. It's not necessary to create a survey for every event and have it completed by every person, but it is important to seek the opinion of each of these groups at some point. You've probably thought of using a survey/questionnaire to get feedback from your volunteers after an event, but what if you also had families complete a short survey together before leaving? You may get feedback from other staff members about the current Sunday morning ministry, but what if you also invited the congregation to sign up for time slots to join you and survey the classes?

A couple years ago at our after-school program, it was Election Day and I decided to allow the kids an opportunity to vote on something for the program. I often ask the opinions of the volunteer leaders, but this was my first time getting feedback from the kids. I decided to start with something easy and fun ... dinner! We created voting ballots with some food choices listed and then blank lines where they could write in other choices. The kids were allowed to mark all of the foods they loved to eat and then turned them into our kitchen crew. We had a lot of fun going through the voting ballots and using those to make the menu for the remainder of the year. It was also exciting when you'd hear the kids yell, "Hey, I voted for this!" as dinner came out of the kitchen. This was a simple way to get feedback on something that mattered to the kids and was a necessary part of our program planning.

THE GOOD, THE BAD, AND THE UGLY

It's also important for you to figure out the best ways to get good feedback from all of the people involved with ministry. Now, when I say "good" I'm not talking about obtaining all positive feedback, I'm talking about obtaining quality feedback. It's easy to get feedback when you know it's going to be positive, but sometimes the most genuine and helpful feedback you receive is not all 5-star ratings. It's also easy to say that you welcome all forms of feedback—positive or negative. The challenging part comes into play when you actually do receive some negative feedback. Trust me, if you're genuinely requesting feedback, some of it will end up being negative no matter how amazing your event or ministry is.

When I started in ministry and began having volunteers fill out surveys, I was extremely offended when they rated anything less than the highest possible rating and when they answered the open-ended questions asking for additional areas of improvement. I took personal offense to any and all remarks made that weren't telling me how perfect and wonderful everything was. Meanwhile, I was telling the volunteers to be open and honest because I valued all opinions. I can't be the only one who has lived this lie at some point in time.

The way I've learned to fix my mindset is by taking a couple extra steps before releasing the survey/questionnaire to a large group. When I create an assessment tool to get feedback about an event, training, program, or the overall ministry, I don't immediately send it to everyone who was involved.

The very first thing I do now is pray over it. The prayer is typically thanking God for the opportunity that we had to share Jesus with children during this event/program. I ask that my mind and heart be opened to ways we could continue making improvements that would bring Him glory and honor. I felt a little silly praying over a survey at first, but it has helped center my thoughts and focus on what's truly important before I start obsessing about the fact that we ran out of popcorn or the table-cloths weren't the right color or three volunteers didn't show up.

After prayer, I then complete the survey myself. This was a step I used to skip because I already knew how I felt about it, right? I ran the event and I made up the questions, but when I made an effort to thoughtfully and honestly answer the questions, I was surprised by my answers sometimes.

The next step is to give the survey to a few key people who served in leadership roles at the event/program. I encourage them to thoughtfully and honestly answer the questions and I've found that most people will follow those instructions. By completing the survey myself first and then adding it to those completed by key leaders, I have an excellent comparison tool as I release it to everyone else who was involved in the event/program. It also allows me to come to terms with the various levels of feedback, resulting in me not being as sensitive to the feedback when it offers suggestions for improvement.

I encourage you to dig into the feedback that is not overly positive and the ones that are downright negative. Depending on your personality, this may be a different experience for you, but it's important no matter how it makes you feel. Some of you may face negative feedback like a challenge to be conquered while others may cry in a corner eating the leftover candy from your event. Some of you may be a little bit in between and face down that mountain of criticism while on a sugar high from your candy binge. Wherever you are on the spectrum, I want you to push yourself to really read the feedback and try to understand it. I'm not saying that you have to agree with all the feedback and immediately put into place all of the changes that were listed. At times there may be missed information that led to a poor rating or someone didn't see the whole picture and thought that something was absent, but it was actually there the whole time. As the leader of this ministry you have a full picture view that not everyone else sees, so some suggestions may not make sense when viewed from your angle.

As you receive submissions, go through and highlight similar responses in one color. If more than one person made the same suggestion, chances are that it's probably an idea worth noting. Then go through with a different color and highlight great suggestions—things that you can't wait to try next time. Finally, go through with a third color and highlight good ideas that just aren't possible because of limitations in a certain area, such as: classroom space, amount of volunteers, lack of financial resources. This is a reminder to follow up with the volunteers to explain why the suggestion wouldn't work or to make changes to one of the limitations to make the idea possible.

SO MANY QUESTIONS, SO LITTLE TIME

My husband and I have been together for nine years and I have had to learn how to interpret his responses. Since the beginning, when I cook something for dinner and ask him how it is, he often said, "Not bad." My brain heard this as, "Wow, this is terrible!" Since that's what I was interpreting by his response, I would never make that dish again. A couple years into our relationship, he asked why I never made a specific dish anymore and I told him that it's because he didn't like it. Well, it turns out he loved it, so I made it again later that week. As he took a bite I asked him how it was and he said, "Not bad." Well, now I was confused. So I asked some questions and found out that while I was interpreting his statement as him not liking it, when he said, "Not bad" he actually meant "This is fantastic!" It's important to learn how to interpret the responses from different people. Your volunteers don't express themselves in identical ways.

Asking the right questions is the most important step of receiving quality feedback, because it will lead you to clear and accurate information. If you're brand new to the idea of getting feedback from anyone in a professional setting, here are a few tips on asking the right questions.

1. WHAT DO YOU WANT TO KNOW?

Before creating a survey or questionnaire, you need to make sure that you actually know what you want to know. It may seem obvious, but it's an important first step. Let's say you're creating a follow-up survey for your Vacation Bible School volunteers. You need to think about what questions would give you useful answers as you wrap up this year and plan for next year.

1. Did you feel adequately trained for your position? *(update your training)*

2. Did you enjoy where you served? Do you plan on returning next year? *(volunteer recruitment)*

3. What was your favorite part of the week? *(encourage the leaders involved in those areas)*

4. Was there enough help in your group? *(how many volunteers are needed next year)*

5. Is there a special story or testimony from the week? *(cast the vision to the congregation about the life change that happens at VBS)*

2. BE SPECIFIC AND VAGUE

That must be a typo, right? No, I actually mean that you need to be specific <u>and</u> vague. When building a survey/questionnaire to get feedback, you need to start with specific questions. They get the attention of the person completing the survey and help them focus back to the event or program in question. After a specific question, you can then move into a vague question that allows them the opportunity to elaborate on the previous question and give more helpful details. Specific questions are also valuable because they give you trackable information so you can see how everyone ranked the Snack Station on a scale of 1-5 and who marked yes/no when asked about being trained adequately. On the other hand, vague questions are helpful because they provide details and allow explanations beyond just a number or selected answer.

3. VARIETY IS THE SPICE OF LIFE

Along with using a balance of specific and vague questions, it's also important to use various types of questions. There are numerous online tools to create surveys (Survey Monkey, Google Forms, Survey Planet). They all allow you to format the survey/questionnaire in different ways and utilize multiple question types. You can use options like multiple choice, open response, drop down boxes, linear scales, and more. These options allow you to ask questions in the best possible way to have your question answered and it keeps the survey more interesting.

4. SHORT AND SWEET

Regardless of who is completing the survey, it does not need to be lengthy. Make sure all questions are answering something that you absolutely need to know. If there are too many, the reader will not take as much time on each question to give thoughtful and thorough answers.

GO AND ASK

Obtaining feedback moves beyond being a desire and instead becomes a need. It is essential to fulfilling your call to lead children into a relationship with Christ. Use the responses from your kids, parents, volunteers, staff members, and church members to spark further conversations. Continue making changes to better teach others and help kids enter into His kingdom.

Emily Hill is the Children's Ministry Director at New Stanton Church in PA. She is a trained social worker with a heart for reaching families throughout the local community. When she's not doing that, you can usually find her scrapbooking and binge-watching reality TV.

chapter 17

DWELL SECURE

Your response determines your reach

BY RACHAEL GROLL

"... but whoever listens to me will dwell secure and will be at ease, without dread of disaster" (Proverbs 1:33, ESV).

HAVE YOU EVER HAD a moment in your life when you were paralyzed by fear? I have. I was sitting in front of the post office, trying to will myself to move. In my lap were 50 letters, stamped, and ready to go; yet, I couldn't quite make myself place them in the mailbox. My daughter, not accustomed to seeing me respond this way, quickly piped up, "Mom, just place the letters in the mailbox. You won't get trampled by an elephant!" Her voice shook me back to reality and I quickly prayed a desperate prayer. "Help, Lord." As I placed the letters where they needed to be, I felt my hands shaking. These were no ordinary letters. No, these were support letters, describing a calling I felt to travel to Africa for an

INSPIRED: UNLOCKING YOUR CREATIVITY

upcoming missions trip. Essentially, sending out those support letters represented my obedience to committing to travel on a trip I never imagined myself making. I reasoned in that parking lot, that if I sent out the letters, I would receive some donations. And if I received donations, I would have to go. And if I went, I was going to either be eaten by a lion, trampled by an elephant, or captured by natives.

Those fears, as absurd as they are, were not the ones keeping me up at night. What kept me up at night was the fear that I would get all the way there ... and fail. This fear of failure is really what had paralyzed me. What could I possibly say to children on the other side of the world? How could I communicate with them when I didn't even speak their language. I looked different, I acted different, and I had no experience working with children living in poverty. Surely, there was someone better qualified to go on this trip. Yet, God had put in my spirit the knowledge that He wanted me to go. I was used to God telling me to do things. Most of the time, they weren't things that scared me. They might make me a little nervous or uncomfortable, but up until this point, God had never told me to do something that terrified me. But this time, God kept pushing my heart in such a way that I could think of little else.

As I faced that mailbox, my fear didn't leave. But, it was a very important piece that started me on a journey to becoming confident as I faced my fear. I was obedient. Despite my fear, I did what God told me to do. Since that time in my life, I've learned what it means to be obedient to God, in all things. Regardless of what things look like in the physical, I have learned that God sees in the spiritual.

In the context of ministry, I think it's so important to consider a few things. You all have moments in your lives when you're paralyzed with fear. Maybe it's a new outreach event or ministry that you sense is needed. Maybe it's disagreeing with someone in your church. Maybe it's firing a volunteer. Or maybe, it's something as simple as trying a new curriculum or object lesson. When I talk to children's pastors across the country, fear of failure seems to loom in the back of too many minds. I often get asked how to deal with this fear, and I believe the answer is found in the book of Proverbs.

Proverbs is a book about wisdom. Initially, you may not think there is a natural connection between fear and wisdom. But stay with me a minute. Wisdom is not the same as knowledge. Yes, as you acquire knowledge, you do tend to become more wise. But biblical wisdom is actually about obedience. As you learn who God is, through your obedience, through your relationship, through His faithfulness, you start to gain a confidence in Him. As you pursue Him, something radical happens in your heart. Fear of the Lord starts to replace fear of the world.

In the first chapter of Proverbs we're introduced to what almost seems like the motto for the book: "The fear of the Lord." The Hebrew word here for "fear" can be translated also to mean "great wonder or awe." Have you ever stood in awe of anything? For me, on that very missions trip, I stood in awe as I looked out over the Great Rift Valley. It was the most beautiful thing I had every laid my eyes on, and I couldn't tear myself away from it. I found myself leaning in, over the peeling white railing, drawn in to this miraculous and breathtaking view.

That awe is similar to what I think of when I hear the words "fear of the Lord" ... not so much the shrinking back in fear, but more of the leaning in feeling of awe. When you know the Lord, really KNOW Him, He draws you in. You can't look away. You can only stare and lean in, because you want to experience more of Him. When you find that place in your relationship with God, the place that comes from knowing and loving Him, the obedience part becomes second nature. You almost don't even think about it. You just arrive in this place where you wholeheartedly trust Him, because you're confident in Him. There is no safer place to be than right where God wants you.

I suspect it may be the same for you once you lean in, in awe of the One who made you.

What is "the fear of failure"? What does that question mean to you? Realize, that **your response will determine your reach.** What I mean by that is simple. If you allow fear to keep you from doing what God is calling you to do, then your reach will stay within the sphere of influence you currently have. However, if your response is one of obedience, using wisdom, confident in the One who calls, despite your fear, then I believe that God will use you in ways you can't even imagine.

Fear. Nervousness. Anxiety. You can get yourself so worked up. God's Word speaks directly to this fear. In Proverbs 1:33 (ESV), it says, "... *but whoever listens to me will dwell secure and will be at ease, without dread of disaster.*"

The word "dwell", in the original text is *yiskon*, meaning "settle down." The original word for secure is *betach*, meaning "confidence." The literal translation of *dwell secure* is that we will *settle down in confidence.* How do you settle down in confidence? Look at the beginning of that verse—*"whoever listens to me."*

There is a connection between what you do and how you feel. If you are obedient to whatever it is that God is calling you to do, you will settle down into the confidence that can only come from your relationship with Him. **Your response determines your reach.**

On that trip I mentioned, God did some incredible things. I walked with families living in a garbage dump, teaching them about the hope we have in Jesus. I prayed with a deaf and mute man and watched, almost dumbfounded, as God healed him right in front of my eyes. I helped lead the son of a local witch doctor to faith in Christ. I saw a young boy, who had been injured severely by an ax to the head, left in a remote area to die, respond as I prayed for him. Within two days his body was restored. We were able to purchase freedom for so many innocent children and mothers from prison, sent for fines of a few dollars. I had the amazing privilege of leading several thousand children to Christ. We were able to rescue women off the street from the human trafficking circles that are too common in impoverished nations. Miracle after miracle, I witnessed the desperate need for the Gospel in the area of the world where God sent me.

If I had not gone, if I had allowed my fear of failure to keep me where I was, God could not have used me to do what He did on that trip. Could God have done it without me? Of course, He could. More than that, He couldn't have done in me what needed to be done.

Before I left, I specifically went to several people and asked them to pray for God to show me how my ministry in Africa could impact my ministry in the States. However, when I was deep in the trenches with hurting people, I was not thinking of home. We were in a section of the country that had children who spoke several different tribal languages, most of which I did not understand. There was a little girl named Sonya who started following me early in the day. She was a believer, and she spoke all the languages the children were speaking. Naturally, she became my interpreter for the day. As we neared the heat of the afternoon, I hiked back to our bus to reapply sunscreen and get some water. We had been told earlier in the day not to allow the children to see us drinking water, or to give any out. However, when I got back off the bus, I realized Sonya had been standing close enough to see through the dark tinted windows. "Mam. Might I trouble you for a bit of your wata?" My heart sank. I was exhausted and thirsty, and I knew she had to be as well. I took her to the rear of the bus, and let her finish the rest of my half empty bottle of water. I hid her behind me so no one would see. She savored every last drop. I could see a physical change in her demeaner. "It has been four days since I have had any wata." Again, my heart sank. As I looked around at, quite literally, the hundreds of children we were surrounded with, I realized that they also had not had any water. They were living in an area that was in deep draught. As this realization sank into my mind, the Holy Spirit whispered something into my heart that I will never forget. *"And if anyone gives even a cup of cold water to one of these little ones who is my disciple, truly I tell you, that person will certainly not lose their reward"* (Matthew 10:42, NIV).

The tears welled up in my eyes. For the first time in my life, I truly understood what those words meant. Then the answer to my prayer back in America came—*This, this is what I want you to do in the States. Love them. Meet their needs. Teach them about Me, the Living Water.*

That moment impacted my ministry here in the U.S. in a foundational way. It became the bedrock on which I built our ministry to the lost and broken children, outside the four walls of our church. In the moments when I feel the pressure to succeed, and the fear of failure starts to creep in, I think about what would've happened if I had let that fear keep me from going on that mission trip. That trip birthed in me something that God continues to use to meet the needs of kids, not only in my community, but in countless communities across the nation.

In the past five years, I have seen innumerable times when God has used me, despite my fear, because of my obedience. As you struggle against your own insecurities, I challenge you to replace your fears with confidence. It is my prayer that you develop the kind of relationship with God that allows you to dwell secure.

THINGS TO CONSIDER:

1. What times in your life have you been paralyzed with fear? If you haven't been paralyzed, have there been things in your life that you have not done because you were afraid? How would your life, your ministry, be different if you started listening to God, no matter what?

2. What is an area of your life that you are not currently being obedient in? How can you start today, moving towards obedience in that area?

3. Take some time to pray through these areas of obedience and fear. Ask God to help you to dwell secure.

Rachael Groll is the Children's and Outreach Pastor at Living Waters Church in Meadville, PA. Her book, *GO*, was published last year, and has served as a resource and inspiration for those seeking to develop and implement their own outreach ministries.

chapter 18

IT'S AN EGG

What to do with a creative idea

BY STEPHANIE CHASE

I T WAS MY FRIDAY OFF. I didn't have to be at the church for one single thing all day or night. Finally, a day all to myself to clear my head, think, dream, and get creative. I headed out the door to do what inspires me—browsing at the nearby bookstore. I surfed the Christian books, scoured the leadership section, and headed to my favorite place—the kids' area. As I entered the brightly colored zone, I noticed a display with three books by the same author. The first hardback arrested my attention immediately: *What Do You Do With An Idea?* by Kobi Yamada.

I quickly stopped and consumed the children's book that every kids' minister, volunteer, pastor, leader needs to read at least once. Why? You have ideas, hundreds of them. They plague you in your sleep, haunt you in the shower, and excite you in moments when you least expect. When these outbursts of creativity hit, what do you do?

DON'T FEAR.

When you first have a creative attack, otherwise known as a new idea, it can be scary. Ideas are different, fresh, out of the ordinary. People may not agree or they may find the concept strange. You don't know who will laugh or make fun. Therefore, your first inclination is to hide your inspiring notions. Do not hide it; instead, take it to God.

Remember the parable of the talents? The manager gave each slave money to manage while he was away. Two made wise investments while the third hid his talent. Why? He was afraid.

Our God is the God of creativity. If you don't believe me, sit in a popular restaurant and watch people. Better yet, look at the kids in your ministry. God is super creative! Not one is exactly the same and each is hard wired in an outstandingly special way.

The creative God of the universe gives people ideas. When a super fun, new idea ignites your heart and mind, take it to God. Seek His confirmation. Write the creative idea on paper. Pray about it. Listen for His response. Ask your Lord, "Is this idea from You? Is this something You want me to pursue?" Listen to His response. Whatever you do, do not bury it, and don't be afraid.

DON'T IGNORE.

Sometimes wild and creative ideas go against the norm. Crossing the Red Sea was not a single thought on the mind of the Israelite slaves. Tearing down the wall of Jericho by marching quietly is a rather bizarre military tactic. God's creative plans for your ministry may be something He calls only you to do.

Whatever you do, don't ignore it. Remember Samuel? 1 Samuel 3 tells how Samuel slept in the temple not far from Eli. When God called Samuel, he did not know it was the Lord. The young boy ran to Eli ready to serve. Eli told the lad to go back to bed. God called Samuel a second time and a third. I don't know about you but I might have been tempted to close my eyes and ignore the voice. When creativity calls, you can't ignore the voice.

What if Samuel had ignored God's call? God's plan? He would have missed anointing David as king, having the tough conversation about Bathsheba, and being used by God in ways that he could not have dreamed.

When God gives you a creative idea, take the idea to a trusted friend. Find your Eli. Begin the conversation by saying, "I have an idea and I want to run it by you." Ideas start out as just that—a creative plan. Often the initial thought will be tweaked and perfected before it is effectively implemented.

Take constructive criticism openly. Listen with intent to improve. Write down your idea and the confidant's suggestions and pray over them. Post the dream in a place where you see it daily. When trustworthy people ask, "Whatcha been up to?" tell them.

What if they say, "That's stupid. It won't work." Don't accept the first "no." Picture the day David appeared on the battlefield where his brothers fought bravely. When Goliath proudly challenged the Israelites, what was David's response? No other soldier dared contest the malicious giant. David experienced God when he fought bears and lions early in his life. The young shepherd knew God could do more than his brothers assumed. When David intended to kill the giant, how did his brothers respond? Eliab grew angry, questioned David's motives, and called him evil.

People are human. We are all sinners. Some may grow angry. Others will not believe you are capable to carry out the creative God-given idea. A few may even condemn you. What if David listened to his brothers?

Don't ignore or abandon the idea in the face of adversity. Go back to God. Pray about it some more. Talk over the responses you received. As you read your Bible daily, notice God's answers in scripture. If God has plans for your creative inspiration, it won't leave you.

My parents told me in my early years of money management training, "If you want to buy something, wait two weeks. If you still want it after two weeks, consider buying it." It's the same with an idea. If that idea is rolling around in your brain for weeks after a major negative response, share it with someone else.

Share the idea with your team. Maybe it's a Sunday school teaching partner, a group of volunteers you serve with, or it could be the kids' ministry staff. Be transparent. Explain your fears or doubts and your super excitement. After revealing your idea, consider the feedback. Take it back to your wrestling mat and grapple with the suggestions. Discover ways the suggestions may help. Throw out thoughts that are secondary to the dream.

I love what John Maxwell said in his book *No Limits*. "Exposure of an idea to the right people + Expression from their different perspectives = Expansion of that idea beyond my personal ability."

If your idea is God-driven, the dream will not leave you. It will tickle your thoughts, appear in your daily routines, and blossom in conversation. Trust God and bring your creative plan to light! Don't hide it and never ignore it. Instead ...

CARE FOR IT.

When I was in middle school homemaking class, we learned to care for babies. How? Each student brought an egg to class. After drawing faces on the fragile ovule, we wrapped the eggs carefully in paper towel. The egg stayed with us for a week. We had to care for it, protect it, feed it, and play with it. Each little egg was our child. Each student whose egg remained whole and undamaged the entire week, got an A. If the poor baby cracked, a C. If it broke, FAIL.

The creative inspiration that wrestles within you must be cared for vigilantly. Treat the dream like a fragile little egg. Nurture the vision God gives you.

ACCEPT IT.

Recognize your idea as valid. Put your faith and trust in God to make the dream a reality. Repeatedly tell yourself, "My idea can happen."

LOVE IT.

Your heart probably skips a beat when you think about your creative idea. Passion oozes from you as you share it with others. Do you know why? Because you love it. You can't stop thinking about it. It consumes you. I am giving you permission to love your idea intimately. Smile, laugh, and dance when you dream about it. Fall in love with your dream.

PROTECT IT.

Creative ideas are quickly rejected by people who resist change. People snub ideas of young, new, and inexperienced leaders. Others will tell you it's impossible simply because they don't understand yet. Protect your baby. Entrust your dream to the trustworthy. Never let a negative, insecure person destroy what God has given you. Your creative idea flows from your heart. *"Guard your heart, for everything you do flows from it"* (Proverbs 4:23, NIV).

FEED IT.

Read, study, and gain knowledge about the idea. Learn from others who are trying similar creative adventures. Watch for people, experiences, and opportunities in your life that relate to your dream. Pursue those prospects.

WORK WITH IT.

Process through every scenario imaginable related to your creative idea. Ask when, where, how, why, who. Answer the questions repeatedly. Test it. Look for ways to practice the idea in small venues. Whatever you do, don't let it sit idly in your brain. Work it.

Why deposit so much care into your creativity? Because this is your creative idea and you are the only one who knows it. You are the one God has called to put this inventive idea in place. You are the one to do it. It's your egg! You must care for it.

The more you care for your dream the more it will make sense. You will see pieces of your inspired creativity begin to fall into place. Like caring for a flower, your dream will grow and blossom as you give it the attention, time, and care it needs.

Pray and seek wise counsel. Talk with your team and others who can make the dream a reality. Massage the idea in your mind. Follow the Spirit's leading. Create a plan to put it into action.

Each creative goal is different. I wish I could tell you the exact plan to put into place, but you are the frontrunner. You lead your ministry, team, volunteers, children, and families to experience the creative vision God has given you.

DREAM BIG, START SMALL.

Creativity breeds big dreams. This is great! Allow your creativity to escort you into God-sized visions. Think beyond your limits and current reality. Pray about God's plan for the ministry, children, and families you lead. Seeking God, discovering creative ideas, and dreaming are the fun part. Once you get clarity on the idea, don't jump in with both feet. Instead, start small. Use a test group or pilot the idea with smaller numbers of people.

God has been moving our ministry to mentor in schools. Creativity struck as we imagined having a free afterschool program at our church for the children we mentor. We loved the creative idea. Our kids' ministry team couldn't wait to get started.

Starting was pivotal though. What was the best and wisest way to have the program? After doing a little research we found two churches hosting similar programs. We piled in my old Suburban and drove to Texarkana. We observed, took notes, and learned ways to adapt and incorporate parts of their system to our idea. Next, we visited a church in San Marcos. Parts of that program resonated with us. We quickly saw components that did not apply to us.

After researching, we created the vision. We met with principals from the schools we mentored, presented the idea, and acquired valuable feedback. Following the meeting, we visited with the leadership of the church. When we received full support and a green light, the afterschool program started.

How many children were in our first group? Twelve. We had to start small. We started with the school most on board. This allowed us time to test the program. We gained valuable insight and made beneficial adjustments. The afterschool program is on its third semester with still 12 children. Why? God has not opened the door for another school until this last month. Pray for us as we prepare to adopt another school this year.

When you start small, you work out the kinks, learn, and adapt. This helps you perfect the creative idea in a safe, practical environment. Dream big, start small is crucial in implementing a new idea.

DEVELOP CLEAR, CONCRETE STEPS.

Write the plan on a hand drawn staircase. The visual illustration will guide you to funnel your creative plan into the succinct actions necessary to bring the creativity to life. The staircase also helps each member of the team recognize how the idea will materialize as you present it.

Think about God's plan for Noah's boat. That was some serious detail. How about God's concise instructions for building the temple? God is a god of order. Turn your creativity into a plan for success by developing clear, concise steps.

There is nothing more fun and exciting than a creative idea. Fresh creativity gives you energy, excitement, and moves ministry to innovative places. If and when God gives you or someone on your team a dream, idea, or creative plan, don't run from it or ignore it, take action. God has plans for creative innovations. Allow Him to use you like He did David, Samuel, Joshua, and Moses. When God plants the spark of creativity in your mind and your heart swells with a newfangled idea, trust God, seek Him, practice the steps we've discussed because God uses simple, new creative ideas to change lives, impact communities, make His name great, minister to families, spread the Gospel, and save His children.

Stephanie Chase is wife to Rick for 25 years, mom of 3 grown kids, and Granny to the cutest little dude ever. She loves leading kids' ministry at Champion Forest Baptist Church in Houston almost as much as eating ice cream, running, and teaching.

chapter 19

EVERYTHING'S GONNA BE ALRIGHT

A look at three uber-creative people

BY AMBER KREIDER

THERE ARE SO MANY creative people in the world. There are people who can create art and music and film and stories and curriculum and events and so many wonderful things that help you experience the world. But there are a special few that are uber-creative. They are the creative elite. They are few and far between, and I am NOT one of them. I have, however, been able to work with and know three of them in my lifetime: Seth, Carrie, and Joe. Being able to watch them create and see their individual processes has helped me grow in my own creativity.

They each are so different from one another, but each is uber-creative in their own way. Seth and Carrie both went to school for youth ministry and served as youth pastors early in their ministry. I worked closely with them several years ago creating a brand new youth conference for our district of churches tucked away in northern Indiana. Seth now works creating big named conferences and events, traveling the world helping produce creative content. Carrie runs an inner city ministry and pastors a small neighborhood church. She creates unique and tailored content every week for her kids, teens, and adults. Joe and I worked together at a summer camp where he designed complex and amazingly fun games. He also is a talented musician, videographer, and writer. I've been able to help him the last few years as he creates music videos, short films, and original music. Most of my help for these uber-creative people has been things like taking notes, sending emails, researching venues, sewing tiny clothes for stop motion characters, and making snacks. It's not usually glamourous work, but has given me such great insight into the mind of the creative elite.

When asked how creative thinking evolves throughout a project, I wrote pages and pages of notes and came up with easily digested steps that someone could follow to help them think creatively. But creativity by nature refuses to adhere to rules or timelines or neatly put together 5-step plans. So, instead of trying to give you a formula, I'm going to tell you things I've learned from Seth, Carrie, and Joe about the creative process. I want to give you encouragement, not advice ... hope, not helpful tips. Each of you come from different places, creating content for different people, different goals, and in different ways.

It's okay if your creative thinking STARTS BIG. Like ridiculously big. Are you planning a circus-themed event? What if you got an elephant to do rides? What if you found a trapeze artist to swing above the sanctuary? I heard from someone that when dreaming, your first reaction should be "Wow!" instead of "How?" Enjoy the dream for a little bit before you have to figure out how it's going to happen. It's okay if your creative process starts at a place bigger than your budget, location, or volunteer base.

Carrie's children's ministry budget is next to nothing, but when she plans her "Kids' Week" (their version of VBS), she often says things like "I want 12 maps printed as giant as possible!" or "Let's decorate the stage with giant grass and flowers so the kids feel like a tiny bug when they walk in!" It's taken me a lot of years to learn to give her space to dream this way. Let her write it down. She's a smart, budget-conscious person. She won't dump the yearly church budget into giant maps for one week, so I don't need to jump in with price breakdowns right away. Taking time to dream big helps you see possibilities. It's okay to dream big!

IT'S OKAY IF YOUR CREATIVE THINKING IS MESSY.

One of the things I did for Seth and Carrie was keep organized notes of their meetings. They both are the type to draw things on napkins, write out ideas all over a piece of paper with a Sharpie, or write a whole day's schedule in pictures on a whiteboard with all the colored markers they can find. I quickly learned to shove all the notes in a box, take pictures of the white boards, and try to type out notes so we could sift through them later. There were ideas that they loved during one meeting and decided against in the next.

I've been part of some event teams that have an organized timeline of things to accomplish. The objective of meeting one was setting the theme. Meeting two focused on setting the schedule, and so on. But Seth and Carrie created a brand new event and didn't have to answer to anyone but each other. So their process got to be a bit more messy. If they decided in the fourth meeting to change up the theme a little, or completely change the schedule two weeks before the event, they did. And while it may have driven some more type A people crazy, it allowed for an incredibly unique and successful conference. They were given the space to be messy—to do things their own way—and it paid off.

Joe does a lot of work in stop motion, which takes crazy amounts of time slowly moving little clay people a little at a time and taking a million snapshots. I've watched him live stream it before and it's fascinating. There's music blasting and all around him are scattered plates of food, sticky notes with complex math notes scribbled on them, laundry, and usually some sort of makeshift bed. It looks like a total trash heap sometimes, but the end product is flawless. You can see on his face that he is focused on the project, and everything else is secondary—designed to keep him alive until his project is finished. He's able to throw all of himself into a project and it pays off in the end.

All three of these people are messy in different ways. It's not always a messy desk. Sometimes, it's a whiteboard full of arrows and things crossed out and sticky notes. Sometimes, it's music blasting in the background and forgetting to eat while they do meticulous work. Sometimes, it's sentences that start one way but end up somewhere different. Often people assume creative people are messy, but I believe it's more the process that can be messy. It's also why it's so helpful for creatives to surround themselves with people who can help them. Find someone who will be able to read your crazy notes and type them up. Find someone who will remind you to sit down and eat in the middle of a big project. It's okay if your process (or brain, or desk, or office) is messy. Just make sure you have good support so you don't get lost in it. (Okay, that was advice, not encouragement; that one's free.)

IT'S OKAY IF YOUR CREATIVE THINKING PRODUCES A CRAZY PLAN.

Just like it's okay to dream big, it's okay if your idea is completely irrational. Seth and Carrie were planning a small youth conference, with a limited budget, and the goal was to keep it very cost effective. But I'll never forget sitting at a coffee shop with them and one of them saying, "Let's get everyone an iPad to use for the weekend!" I remember laughing out loud, and them turning to me with that "It's ridiculous but we're going to make it happen" twinkle in their eyes I've come to recognize so well. The more we planned the event, the more important it became to give the attendees access to the technology an iPad could provide. It was ridiculous! We did not have the budget for it. But we made it happen.

One time, Joe was making a music video where he wanted to get a shot of people running through a field with flash lights from high above. We found a field, with a climbing tower next to it that he could film from. The only problem? It was the dead of winter in Indiana, and there was a good two feet of snow in the field. But Joe had an idea in his head, and so I'll never forget pulling on boots, and extra layers, and "running" through two feet of snow in a field. It turned out awesome!

Sometimes, you get ideas in your head that sound ridiculous when you say them out loud. Sometimes, those are the best kind. Do not be discouraged by raised eyebrows. If it's important to your overall vision, dig your heels in.

IT'S OKAY IF YOUR CREATIVE THINKING SLIMS DOWN YOUR IDEA.

Confession ... not every student got an iPad at the conference. We ended up being able to afford one for very 10-12 students. And Carrie's giant maps? We ended up with fewer than she wanted, and they were slightly smaller than she first envisioned. For a few videos, Joe has needed to match exact outfits of real people to their tiny clay counterparts. He gave me pictures of people, and asked me to sew tiny matching outfits. Fun fact, I am NOT a seamstress, so I often buy doll clothes and alter them to fit. The truth is, we do work with budgets and facilities and limited volunteers. So don't be discouraged if your big dreams and crazy ideas get slimmed down a little.

The truth is, you are called to be good stewards of the resources God has entrusted you with. It's healthy and wise for you to let things go that don't really matter. I remember telling an intern that at every event I plan there's at least one great idea that ends up not making it to the end, because I run out of budget and there's simply no time to put it together. You need to think of your projects like you would yourself. Sometimes you need to trim the fat a little to be healthy and capable of accomplishing your goals.

IT'S OKAY IF YOUR IDEA CHANGES.

This year for VBS, I dreamed up this idea to use a farmhouse kitchen kind of theme and talk about growing healthy. I wanted to relate the idea of eating healthy foods to growing strong bodies to filling our hearts with healthy spiritual disciplines that would grow stronger faith. I imagined a farmhouse kitchen on the stage, with a big island that the teacher would teach behind as they cooked.

But this was the first year I put together a team of people to help with VBS. I had talented, capable people in charge of different areas, helping me develop the whole thing from the ground up. It was amazing to work, dream, and plan alongside a team. The more we talked and planned, the more the idea changed from a farmhouse kitchen full of food, to a garden full of plants, and talking about growing strong healthy "roots." Once VBS rolled around we had the stage decorated like a backyard garden, the "potting shed" set up for crafts, and a pop-up garden on our front lawn filled with edible plants and beautiful flowers. I looked around one night before we started, and for a moment, I mourned my original idea of a farmhouse kitchen. But I quickly reminded myself that good ideas adapt and evolve to work with the people, places, and resources afforded to us. It was a great success, beautifully executed, and something I really believe God wanted to teach our kids in this time. If you're tempted to look at a project and feel discouraged that it's not what you originally dreamed, remember that the creative process demands adaptation.

The simple fact is that creative thinking evolves throughout a project for all of us. It will flow and change and shrink and grow. It will be messy and crazy and will look different for all of you. There may be a point when your desk is covered in scraps of paper with ideas and sketches. There may be a point when you forget to eat lunch because you're so focused. There may be a point when your team or boss looks at you like you're crazy. There may be a point when you have to shave off some of the unnecessary ideas to fit your budget. Whatever your process looks like, stay focused on your vision and your goals, and you will succeed.

Amber Kreider is the Children's Ministry Director at a neighborhood church in South Bend, IN. She loves being able to wear novelty T-shirts to work, and getting the pastors to dress up in costume. It's her desire to create a space for kids to learn to love Jesus and the local church, all while embracing the abundance of whimsy and joy that God has intentionally created them with. She also loves coffee, sci-fi, and filling her bike basket with snacks and riding around the neighborhood.

chapter 20

CREATING THE WOW!
Fun with environments

BY JORDAN DAVIS

I F I WERE TO RATE MY TOP favorite things in children's ministry I would have to say that, after leading and baptizing kids in the name of Jesus, my second favorite thing would be creating environments for kids to enjoy. Creative environments have always been a top priority of mine. Seeing the kids walk in for the first time to a newly decorated space with a smile and a wow on their faces brings me great joy. From the facility as a whole, to a newly decorated stage depicting the theme of the month, it's all worth it. I've learned a few lessons (some the hard way) that I would love to share with you.

The first and most important lesson that caused me many long days and sleepless nights is this: No matter why you are creating, you must create out of need and not want.

I've spent countless hours trying to mimic an item or design that I wanted so badly, only to realize that it didn't even fit into our ministry. When I say fit, I don't mean size or color or theme. I mean, it didn't fit our ministry, the way I taught, and often it wouldn't fit the way that our kids needed to learn. What you bring to the table in your kids' ministry is not only who you are but also whom your ministry is geared towards.

In my first few years, I visited different churches, attended a variety of conferences, and surfed the web for different environmental ideas. It left me wanting more than needing. I simply wanted to do and have whatever seemed to be working so well for the other guys. It was only after many hours of working on copying what they had created, that I realized that this great thing would not even work for us, because this great thing was really just a want and not a need. You want your kids to have the WOW factor as they enter your environments. You go to conferences or visit a larger church and see something amazing. As an adult you experience that same WOW factor that you want your students to have, so you try to duplicate that in your facility. But the truth is, you don't need it. You're not that church and you can't do what they do, just as they can't do what you do. Your environment has to meet your needs and not just your wants.

About five years ago I sat at a table with several children's pastors from across the country and we each took five minutes to describe the ministries that we came from, what part of the country we were in, how many kids, and what type of ministry we ran. I will never forget our conversation afterwards. While listening to each person share, we all grasped on to something from each person and we wanted that thing. One pastor had a thriving volunteer group (yes, that can happen), another a growing outreach ministry, and another a great facility. All of us would have loved someone else's problem. What I began to see is that it is obvious, we are all in different bodies of believers and run different ministries that often reflect our own personalities and leadership styles.

I want you to think about creativity in the same way. My personality sees the big picture. I am not focused on the details.

This is also how I create. I tend to think big picture and let the details work themselves out. I love decorating from the front door all the way in to the stage. But if you ask me to create a craft, I will hand you a brown bag and a crayon. That's just not how God created me; I don't see the small details.

This leads me to the second lesson I've learned about creating environments for kids. Create from your personality and partner with others to complete the project.

It really is okay to dream with a team. If you're not a big picture person, then gather a big picture person on your design team (even if the team only consists of you and them). You think better when you think together. My wife is a detail person. I can spend hours and hours creating an amazing environment and she can walk in and offer a suggestion or two that can elevate it to an entirely new level. Create from your personality and partner with others to get the WOW response.

When creating environments as a whole, here are a few things you must know.

1. YOUR ENVIRONMENT STARTS AS SOON AS YOU WALK IN.

I've been to many facilities that almost feel like you're walking into a funeral home as you enter the kids' area. For a new child, if a hallway is blank, stark, and uninviting, then they may come into your space a little more apprehensively.

Maybe you come from a facility where you're not given license to decorate as you please. I would like to give a few simple ideas. First, color! Even if you cannot do crazy colors on the walls, perhaps a nice soft color would liven up the area or add a colorful poster or two. Perhaps you don't have the ability to decorate as you would like. How about adding some friendly, clean-cut signage? How about a bulletin board decorated with this month's theme, verse, or upcoming event information?

Second, music! Canned music is a great way to add some life to your environment. Finally, add greeters. Anywhere there may be a gloomy part of the building leading to your ministry, place a greater to engage the students before they even enter your environment. A bright and shiny volunteer is worth more than anything you can buy on Amazon. Often, the way a child enters your environment will set the course for how they interact with your lesson.

2. BRANDING IS EVERYTHING!

Branding is everywhere and on everything. The biggest corporations in the world have influenced us on this. Church is no different and your logo matters! One of the ways you know you are succeeding in your town is if your local schools know who you are by the name and logo of your kids' ministry. One of my ministry goals has been to saturate the market (my kids' schools) with who we are as a church, from t-shirts to invite cards. I want my students talking about this place that they love.

A great example of this is an event from my previous ministry called Kidsfest. Kidsfest is a free festival put on by the area churches. Thousands of people from our town poured into the city park for a 6-hour festival on the first Saturday of July. Weeks before the event, we put out lime green signs all over town and volunteers began wearing the lime green shirts with our logo on them. People stopped volunteers and asked for information on this year's event, anticipating the return of the great festival. We would literally be painting the town lime green with our advertising. That logo was associated with people who could be trusted, people who would share the Gospel in a new and exciting way, and church people who knew how to have fun.

In the same way, your kids' ministry logo, whether you like it or not, partially defines who you are as a ministry. Make sure your logo is not only relevant but also represents who you are. Once you have it, plaster it everywhere!

3. DESIGNATED AREAS CREATE DISCIPLINE.

The first children's ministry room I was given to decorate, in a little town in Kentucky, was a 10' x 20' room. I quickly realized how small of a space it was and how non-functional a multi-purpose room could be if the spaces were not properly defined. It is vital, if at all possible, to make sure you have a designated space for different parts of your service and/or ministry. A place designated for fun may not be a great place to worship or learn.

A lot of times our ministries call for crazy awesome games, but then we expect the kids to immediately sit down and be quiet and ready to listen. That will not, and should not happen, for the sanity of all involved. But, what if you can move over 5 feet in the room to a designated "sitting area" and reset your environment. Simply by changing your tone, music, and lighting you will have a whole new group of attentive kids. Designate parts of your room for loud times and quiet times. If space allows even a place for large groups and small groups.

4. DREAM BIG. PRAY BIGGER.

I've been told that I have a knack at getting free items donated for ministry. I don't say that to toot my own horn, but really, here's the secret. You have to continually cast vision for what you want the space to look like, what you want the service to sound like, what you want your environment to feel like. When people hear your vision, they will also open their minds and dream along with you. For me, people often saw items in the community and then they asked if I could use it or need if for a project I may be envisioning.

I couldn't talk about dreaming big without reminding you to pray bigger. Continue to plead with God to enlarge your reach, broaden your ideas, and shine light on your dreams. When you ask God to be the brains behind your creativity, you should never be surprised.

Eight years ago, I had just left the gym and happened to have the radio on early in the morning when an advertisement came on about our local mall giving away their indoor playground. I caught most of it while I was driving and knew there was an application process. Honestly, I laughed a little, "How cool would that be to have a playground inside our space! Okay God." I shared the vision with our leaders and we dove into the process of applying. Almost two months later, we were awarded the playground and were standing at the bottom of our 2-story building trying to figure out how to get a 500 pound hot dog and watermelon slide up the stairs to our kids' environment. When you ask God for something big, be ready to put all your might into it.

5. DON'T BE A SLAVE TO A BUDGET.

This lesson really goes with dreaming big, but I want to be clear. Some of the greatest creative elements I've ever done were cheap. Time and vision create wonder. I wonder how Noah felt building the ark. He had God's inspired vision and used his hands to design it. You are given complex brains and strong hands, so use them to create.

An old-school overhead with a pencil, some free scrap cardboard, and a few bottles of paint can completely change an environment. Paint is cheap and can be an easy way to change your look each month. Couple your need for props with the talent in your church and you have something amazing going. Put something on your social media thread asking if your church workers have a talent for art or a passion for kids. You'll be surprised who comes forward to help.

6. DUMPSTER DIVING IS A MUST!

Think outside the box for every project you do. Someone else's trash could be your treasure. It may no longer function well for its original use, but you see it fulfilling an entirely new purpose. I will never forget the time I was looking for Lego tables for my large group room. I worked part-time at a mall and witnessed Victoria Secret (yes, you read that right) throwing away underwear tables. They were perfect! It was a table with sides, and were only as tall as a child. What better table could you come up with to hold Legos?

7. DON'T LIMIT YOURSELF.

A really hard lesson to learn is that sometimes your vast creative mind will limit your outcome. One trend that has hurt many environments is that of a permanent solid theme. Once you have a set theme for your building you are locked in for the long haul. I challenge you to create a place that is creative, yet diverse. Spend more time changing your environment for the series you are in and less time making a city out of the rooms. In the long run, it's usually cheaper and by being able to change things up, you also create an excitement with the kids. They can have new WOW experiences over and over each month as the themes change.

8. GET ON THEIR (YOUR STUDENTS') LEVEL.

Get on your knees and walk around as if you were one of your students. What do they see? How do they see it? What does your environment look like from the eyes of your children? Are they invited in or simply bystanders on your creative journey?

What your environment boils down to is: How does your environment reach children? Is it inviting? Is it engaging? Is your environment something that will change a child's eternity? My prayer is that you ask the God who gives creativity for a new, fresh vision for your environment.

Jordan Davis is a fun-loving, big guy, in a kids' world. He loves seeing kids grow into their own personal knowledge and understanding of a relationship with Jesus. He and his wife, Kati, are raising 3 young boys to be great men of God and leaders in the Kingdom.

chapter 21

BIG IMPACT,
SMALL BUDGET

One prop at a time

BY KEN NEFF

HAVE YOU EVER WALKED into a place, any place, and been in awe of your surroundings? All you could say was the 3-letter word that we often associate with a childhood experience, "WOW!" Theme parks all over the world have been creating these atmospheres to give you the experience of a lifetime, every time. The leader of the pack in my opinion is Disney. Walt knew a thing or two about the "WOW" factor. So why can't we as the church do the same thing? I'm not talking about building a Christian theme park, although that might not be a bad idea. I'm talking about capturing your kids, the kids down the street, and the kids across town. Either the world is going to capture their attention or the church is. So think big, dream big, and ask the Creator of the Universe to help you. After all, you couldn't ask for a better artist.

This is where I think stage designs and props are very important for the church and especially in the children's ministry, because the designs tell a story and give children a visual taste of what your children's ministry is all about. After all, Jesus was a storyteller and gave a visual, figuratively speaking, every time He told a parable to His audience. What are your kids saying when they walk into their rooms at service time? Are they staring at a blank wall, a fixed theme, or just plain out of the box decor as it relates to the atmosphere of their church experience.

Humans are wired to be visually stimulated, whether it's the food you eat, the cars you buy, or just the common recognition through TV commercials and products. This starts as babies when you're mesmerized by the mobile placed above the crib. So when a stage design is well thought out with color, prop arrangement, size, lighting, along with other elements like video and sound, it all comes together for a "WOW" and all for God's glory.

So make your children's ministry eye appealing and relational to your kids. Don't be afraid to change it up from time to time, giving it a fresh look. You're probably thinking, "But Disney World doesn't change Main St. every month." No they don't, but then again, most people don't go to the theme park every weekend and possibly midweek, too. So when you do go, even if it's once a year, it all looks fresh and exciting to you all over again. Unless you have a secret that you need to share with the rest of the kidmin world, you're saying, "But I don't have a budget like Disney." Neither do I, and we'll get to that in a few moments.

However, after speaking with children's pastors, leaders, and teachers all over the country, I continue to hear these words time and time again. "I'm not creative enough!" Oh, but you are. Take out the "not" in that statement, then say it again, "I'm creative enough." Like any of the gifts and talents you have received from God, you are more gifted in some areas and more challenged in others. Personally, I don't like to use the word "weaker," because it tends to give a preconceived stigma of yourself. So let's use the word "challenged." You all have challenges even in your most gifted areas. I have absolutely no construction or art background at all, so I fully rely on God when it comes to stage designs.

Since you are all made in the image of God, you all have it in you; it just needs to be pulled out and exercised. You all have the same muscles. It's just that some people exercise them more so those muscles are more developed. The same goes true with our creative muscle. You need to stop staring at the gym from the parking lot and get in the front door. Like anything that you need to develop, start out slow. When it comes to creative designs for a stage or just a prop, start out slow and work your way up to the next level. Feeling overwhelmed and tackling a task too big will quickly lead to discouragement and the idea that stage designs and props are not for you, but for the other church. Believe me, I've been there with blood, sweat, and tears. Trust me, they were not tears of joy. I've been at the church until midnight or later on a Saturday night trying to get the stage completed for service. So work that creative muscle one day at a time and let God be your trainer.

Based on these concepts, every calendar month, along with some amazing volunteers I create a new stage design in our elementary sanctuary for under $100.00 to coincide with our curriculum series that we write. This is not a think-of-an-idea-today and build-it-tomorrow thing. There's a lot of pre-planning. The more pre-planning the easier it is, and the friendlier on your budget it will be, which will add even more excitement to your project. You're working with kids so you need excitement displayed on your stage and bigger-than-life props.

What does a theme look like from paper to stage? I'm glad you asked. Start with prayer and let God impart to you what He wants. Get it down on a napkin, paper, or digital device. The Bible tells us *"Where there is no vision, the people are unrestrained"* (Proverbs 29:18, NASB). So don't try to keep it all in your head or you're sure to lose some of it. Focus brings a clearer picture like that on a camera.

With your design concept in mind, the fun part starts. Here are a few things to keep in mind when shopping at a retail store or flea market. I buy copious amounts of pool noodles at the end of summer when they hit the clearance rack, as well as marked down fabric, and mis-tinted paint that stores try to get rid of for less than half off. I also purchase Christmas lights that can be used for all kinds of things, such as: putting lights on a Ferris wheel, making a campfire glow, or a giant starfish shine. At 50-75% off, they almost seem to shine brighter.

I suggest you build a relationship with your local carpet stores, not just for carpet, but for the carpet tubes themselves. They make great giant pencils, paintbrushes, Link-N-Logs, pine trees or chopped up for cannons on your pirate ship. Don't forget your local big box stores, for what else, big boxes from appliances, wooden pallets, or slightly damaged products that they are likely to discount for you.

Let your congregation know what your needs are, and you'll be amazed at what you can borrow for your design. I used social media and requested a canoe, and within two minutes a church member responded. If doing a camping theme, see if someone has a tent, canoe, fishing poles, and sleeping bags. Add some trees, a dock, and water. You'll have a stage design without dipping deep into your budget.

One last thing before you put the hammer to the nail or the brush to the paint. Think big, because you serve a big God. You can create a design on a dime to get the attention of your kids while sharing the Gospel in a unique way that they will never forget.

Ken Neff is a husband and ministry partner to his wife, Andrea, father to Chris and founder/president at Fun Factory Ministries. Ken is a camp/conference speaker, children's ministry trainer, and loves to bring the Bible to life with visual objects that are bigger than life.

chapter 22

IF IT'S AVAILABLE, USE IT!

Technology in kidmin

BY JACK HENRY

IT'S SUNDAY AND I'M SO EXCITED! I arrived early to get everything ready. I went to the closet and pulled out the long chair rack and began to set up the brown metal chairs. (Anyone remember how much noise they made moving them around?) I prayed for each one as that chair represented a child who would soon sit there and learn about Jesus. Many of the chairs were old and had some rust. After setting up about 60 chairs, perfectly aligned of course (although they would soon be greatly disrupted), I brought out THE TABLE! We had one table designated for kids' church. I went back to the closet and got out our state of the art Radio Shack sound equipment. We had two speakers and two mics ... all corded, of course. After I got all of that set up and made sure the mics worked (a little squealing was okay), I went back to get the main two things that we were so proud of: our huge boom box with a cassette player and our overhead projector! I can feel your excitement. Back to the closet (yes, we had a closet and yes it was shared) to get our homemade puppet stage. The puppets were a bit rough and worn but hey, they got the job done. I never had a kid complain. I got out our music cassettes and found the songs we were doing that day. I wrote down the number count that showed on the top of the player. This allowed me to fast forward to where we needed to be. But when you went past the song you had to rewind a bit. Some songs were on different tapes so that made all this more challenging! Most of the time when you hit "Play", you endured the last 5 seconds of the previous song until the one you wanted started playing. The kids didn't seem to mind. It made that funny sound through the speakers and they loved it. Okay! Old metal chairs set up. Check! Overhead projector and plastic sheets with lyrics. Check! Radio Shack sound system. Check! Two mics hot, and I mean hot, and ready to go. Check! Boom box with all my numbers ready to go. Check! Puppet stage and puppets. Check! Did I mention that I had my guitar? Oh yes. I plugged it right into the 4-channel sound system and played along with the music, even though all that sound would, at times, shut the system down! I liked it loud but the sound system fought me on that. Soon the kids arrived and we began worship. It was awesome! We saw tons of lives change back in that day and we used the technology that was available and affordable. Many of those kids are in ministry today! Praise God for His supply.

Fast forward. What you just read was my Sunday routine from back in 1982. Kids did not show up with their iPods, iPads, and cell phones, waiting to see all the cool video stuff on the big screens. It was a simpler time.

FACTOID: WE USED WHAT WE HAD FOR THE DAY AND IT WORKED!

We used what was available! But that day has gone ... forever! We are in a new generation, folks. Although much has changed, the one thing that has not changed is what I just said:

We used what was available! That's the key. If you're going to attract and keep the kids coming, as well as keep parents happy, you need to be as up to date as possible on what's available and use it in your ministry. Is technology important? Your answer needs to be yes, at least if you want to keep them coming. You can either see this trend (that's here to stay) as a problem or embrace it and use it to enhance your ministry.

Children are more tech-savvy than ever. Unfortunately, some churches view this trend as a distraction rather than an opportunity. Well, here are three reasons that show us why technology is a great teaching tool for your kids' ministry.

KIDS LOVE TECHNOLOGY

Duh, right? Studies show that children, right from 6-month-old babies to teens, enjoy engaging on mobile apps and the Internet. In fact, 25% of children under 5 years use the Internet at least once a week, while kids ages 8-10 spend 5.5 hours each day playing games or watching videos. Given these numbers, it is evident that modern-day kids love using technology. Kids love technology. Adults as well.

EDUCATIONAL MOBILE APPS HAVE A POSITIVE IMPACT ON KIDS

Despite the age-old argument about the negative effects of technology on children, 71% of parents believe that mobile devices provide new learning opportunities for their kids. Not only that, they say that educational mobile apps promote curiosity, teach reading, and foster creativity. For example, the Bible App for Kids incorporates picture puzzles, multiple choice questions, and read-on-your-own stories, to help kids develop skills such as problem-solving, memory, and reading. More importantly, this app uses creative techniques to effectively teach God's Word to the little ones. If you haven't yet checked it out you should. Push your leaders and parents to as well.

One of my favorite apps is Right Now Media. It is slammed full of content that communicates to every age group. I use it every week in ministry. We drive parents to it for family devotions and the church as a whole uses it for life groups. Amazing.

FACTOID: TECHNOLOGY IMPROVES LEARNING IN CLASSROOMS

A growing number of schools are embracing technology-friendly methods for teaching. In fact, 74% of educators support the use of technology in their classrooms. Perhaps this is because educational technology, such as mobile apps, serves a twofold purpose: helps teachers reinforce the curriculum and motivate kids to learn.

Schools are increasingly realizing that the 21st-century kids need to be taught using 21st-century tools. Now that makes sense! Back in 1982 I used what was current and the kids identified with it and they learned. Even back in the day, I always did my best to stay current and I raised money and fought to make sure we had the best. It made a huge difference and we had great numbers. Is it always about the numbers? No, but every number represents a child's life and soul. I want them and I want to keep them!

Are you making the most of modern-day technology to teach the kids in your church? If you aren't, kids very well may ask their parents to try another ministry that is doing so. The world is doing its best to steal the minds and souls of our kids through technology! The church needs to step it up, because we're in a heated competition, not with other churches, but with the world. Maybe you can't have everything you want at once, but you have to start somewhere. Let me give you some of these *"somewhere"* things.

1. **Check in.** Keeping kids secure is of supreme importance in kids' ministry. No doubt it can certainly be done through various low-tech solutions, but if you're able, consider how you can use tech to make this process as

secure and efficient as possible. Also, don't miss opportunities to incorporate tech to communicate with parents during the check-in and check-out times. Consider playing videos or slideshows detailing upcoming events, what is being taught that day, and ministry highlights as well. I like to put a large TV on a cart at check-in and run short, fun commercials of what's going on in kids' ministry. Everyone loves it! I have actually seen an increase of attendance at our events and services.

2. **Volunteer Training.** Hard to get volunteers to come to training? Take the training to them. Grab a camera or just use your phone. Record your training. Post it online. Send the link to your volunteers. Follow up with discussion questions when you meet before the weekend service. It's not difficult to create a culture of learning by providing several tech-related delivery platforms. Consider how you can encourage leaders and parents to use tablets to view training content. People are always on the go these days, so you have to create ways to train them as they are "going." I love to make training videos for my leaders that are no more than four minutes in length and full of rich content. We also create content for parents. You can't raise their children, but you can come alongside them and give encouragement by equipping them and helping them walk the path. You need to be helping parents be the spiritual leaders for their kids by providing parenting tips videos. You can then send them the link to watch the video. You can easily design a Facebook page to communicate with parents. Texting is popular: 98% of text messages get read! This is a great way to connect and communicate with parents. If it's available, use it.

3. **Online Registrations and Donations.** Technology is a great tool for registration for camps, events, classes, dedications, and everything else. I don't know what I would do without it! This year, 80% of VBS kids signed

up online! We also created an Amazon link where people could go and buy requested items we needed for VBS and they come straight to the church! We reached the 90% mark this year in donations! Can I get an "Amen" somebody? We made it easy for them to do it, so they did it!

4. **Classrooms.** Videos and music are often used in kids' curricula and the dropping cost of televisions and other equipment makes it possible even for smaller churches to use these resources to help teach kids. If installing televisions in each room is out of reach because of cost or you are in a portable context, consider laptops as an alternative. Having screens in the classrooms intensifies the learning and creates an atmosphere of excitement with this generation. Teachers use their screens each week here at Marcus Point for Right Now Media content that greatly enhances their teaching! Classes are growing as a result, because the kids want to be there.

5. **Data for Ministry.** A database allows you to keep contact information and records for families. It also helps you track the spiritual growth steps of kids and families. A database is great for so much more than tracking contact information and attendance. Many databases will also generate automatic reports based on parameters you set up, such as when a kid has missed two weeks in a row. Some will go a step further and even generate automatic emails or letters to be printed. Imagine using technology to automatically contact your teachers letting them know their kids who have missed and reminding them to give each absent kid a call ... without you needing to do anything. I'm not kidding when I tell you that we're experts at collecting data from people. We have a ton of people who we invite to events throughout the year and many show up. As I am writing this, we just finished our first day of VBS. We had 682 show up, mainly due to data we had collected from other events. The number will

grow throughout the week and this means more lives touched and changed by the Gospel!

6. **Media Presentations.** Today's kids are very visual. Programs like PowerPoint, Pro Presenter, Keynote, and Media Shout are all great options for communicating visually with kids. So many cool options exist! Motion backgrounds. Countdowns. Sound effects. Sound effects on slides go a loooooong way. There are tons of free ones (and legal) on YouTube. You need to make your presentations come alive in order to reach out and grab your listeners! Look at what is in the world that you compete with? This is how kids today learn.

FACTOID: TECHNOLOGY CONTINUES TO RESHAPE EDUCATION SYSTEMS AROUND THE WORLD!

The changes will eventually reach Christian education, as well. Sadly, church normally lags behind a few years. Often this is due to resistance to change or insufficient resources needed to expedite the changes. That being said, here are three changes that are taking place in the education realm. Get ready children's ministries ... it's coming your way, too.

COMPUTER GAME-BASED LEARNING

As game-based learning becomes more accepted and effective, teachers will use it more often in classrooms. Churches will eventually use computer games and apps as a method to teach Bible stories and truths.

E-BOOKS

Schools will continue to move away from print books and embrace e-books. Kids will bring the Bible to church on their mobile device instead of carrying it in print form. The Church needs to take a lesson here.

BRING YOUR OWN DEVICE

The "bring your own device" movement will gain popularity as schools realize they can save big bucks by allowing students to use their personal devices in the classroom. Kids will explore Bible lessons and truths on their devices as teachers facilitate. I do allow kids to bring in their devices but only if they use it for reasons we give. If we spot a child playing games, they are asked to put it away. Many times, we will take it and give it back to the parents, telling them that we do allow them but only if they use it for the Bible app and a few other things we allow.

Are you already using any of these in your children's ministry? How?

How do you think these trends will change the way you do children's ministry?

What other technology trends do you see coming to children's ministry?

Do you need help in this area of technology? Feel free to reach out to me at oldkidspastor@gmail.com.

Technology. It's available, so use it! Blessings!

Jack Henry is a lifetime kids' pastor now serving his 35th year. The mind is willing but the body is weak, so he's going back to the gym to get caught up with his mind! He loves being a part of life change!

chapter 23

CREATIVELY ADDRESSING THE MULTI-AGED CLASSROOM

Overcoming the challenges to reap the rewards

BY AMBER PIKE

EVERY AGE GROUP OF CHILDREN presents its own unique set of challenges, and at times, difficulties. Having a classroom full of children of mixed ages can present an even bigger set of challenges. In typical mixed-age children's ministries, the children range from preschool (age 4) to 5th or 6th grade (age 11 or 12). It's a wide range full of learning and spiritual differences, and after 10 years of leading multi-aged children's ministry, I have seen first-hand the difficulties and challenges it can present. More than the challenges, though, I have seen the blessings and the rewards a multi-aged classroom can bring.

THE CHALLENGES

It can be easy to get discouraged with a multi-aged classroom. When part of your class is disengaged, causing a distraction ending with the whole class erupting in chaos, it can lead to frustration, discouragement, and disappointment. For some people, the challenges seem overwhelming and insurmountable, but if you're aware of what the challenges are, it can help you proactively and effectively combat them.

Attention spans are at different lengths. Obviously a 4-year-old cannot sit and listen to a 20-minute message like a 5th or 6th grader can. Attention spans can be one of the biggest challenges a multi-aged classroom will face. Every age group and every child has to stay engaged at the same time, or you have lost control of the class.

Teaching at everyone's level is impossible. When you have a multi-aged classroom, there is no way to teach to everyone's level at the same time. Different aged children are at vastly different academic, mental, and spiritual levels. The same is true for any classroom setting, even children of the same grade and age, but the difference is greater for the multi-aged classroom. Since there is no way to teach to everyone's level at once, you have to choose where your lesson will be aimed. Not every child will be at their full learning potential, but if you aim your lesson correctly, every child will be able to learn.

Multiple reading levels can create difficulties. Activities involving reading and writing can be challenging when you have children on both ends of the age spectrum. A preschooler or kindergartener, most likely, cannot read and write yet, so activities involving such are lost on them. They often become frustrated, distracted, or cause a disruption due to their inability to participate in the activity. Leaders must find a way to keep young children engaged during activities that require reading and writing.

Multiple levels of spiritual maturity affect the lesson. Though any room full of children has different levels of spiritual maturity, in a multi-aged classroom the differences are greater. Not only is each child at a different level of maturity in their walk with Christ, but each age group is (typically) limited to the level of biblical understanding they are capable of. There are some concepts a preschooler is just not capable of grasping yet, such as abstract or metaphorical thinking. Staying only on a preschooler's level of simple basic foundational Bible truths could easily bore the older children, though, leading to distraction. Leaders must make sure they are reaching all ages with their phrasing and teaching while striving to reach many levels of biblical learning.

THE REWARDS

There are days when the challenges that must be overcome when leading a multi-aged classroom seem difficult. You might even have days when it feels like no one got a thing from the day's lesson. Despite the difficulties, I have come to find that the rewards and blessings far outnumber the challenges.

Friendship and connectivity between the whole group is encouraged. When the classroom is full of children from all different ages, the whole group begins to grow closer. The younger children latch on to their favorite older kids, often idolizing and emulating their actions, while the older children naturally step into a helper and leadership role. Oftentimes, unlikely friendships are formed because of the diversity in age groups.

Children will still form pairs and groupings of close friends within the group, but a tight knit community is being formed around them. Kids are kids, and there will always be best friends. In addition to these groups of best friends, you will see that tolerance, patience, and connectivity will abound throughout the whole group.

Learning opportunities are greater for all ages. More opportunities for growth, aside from teacher-led instruction, are created in this setting. The younger children have the opportunity to witness or possibly participate in things they would not normally see and do because of their age.

Take for instance the sacraments of baptism and the Lord's Supper. In a class of preschoolers alone, there isn't typically a high rate of baptisms amongst those children nor are many of them typically partaking in the Lord's Supper. In the multi-aged classroom, however, the opportunity for the younger children to witness the older children participating in these sacraments is greater. When a younger child sees their older friend being baptized, it opens the door to a great discussion and plants the seeds.

The learning opportunities are not limited to the younger children alone, however. In a class with younger children, the older kids learn a lot about themselves. Through helping with the younger children and being the examples, the older children learn about their giftedness, their leadership skills, and are able to learn through service. They are encouraged to practice patience, compassion, and self-control, and they possibly see the fruits they are lacking in.

By having the opportunity to set the example for the younger children, the older children in the room sometimes become the teachers and helpers. In addition to the growth and skills that alone brings to the table, this helps to keep the older children who are ready to move on to youth group engaged. If they are busy serving and leading, the older children have less time and inclination to act up or cause a distraction.

THE MISCONCEPTIONS

One of the biggest misconceptions about teaching to a classroom with children of all ages is that you have to dumb it down so much that you end up losing the interest of the older children. That is simply not true. Heavy theological concepts and even practical apologetics can be taught to children of all ages. Preschoolers are capable of comprehending so much!

You can teach in such a way that everyone in the room has the opportunity to learn. It is entirely possible to keep the attention of all ages at the same time. You do not have to pick and choose which age group you will teach to, while the rest of the children are just along for the ride. When done properly, multi-aged classroom teaching does not have to be an unsurmountable challenge, but it can truly be a blessing to all involved, both leaders and children.

PRACTICAL FOUNDATIONS OF THE MULTI-AGED CLASSROOM

So how does a multi-aged classroom look? How should lessons be set up to make things run smoothly, keeping all children engaged? Understanding and including these practical foundations with each lesson will help to make your multi-aged classroom a possibility.

Teach to the oldest boy. You've heard it before, but it rings true. To capture the greatest number of children, your lesson needs to be aimed at the oldest boy in the room. Older girls will typically go along with whatever the lesson entails, regardless if they particularly enjoy it or not, while older boys are harder to please. The "cool factor" plays a huge roll in whether or not boys will participate.

One time in my ministry, I showed a clip from a Veggie Tales movie. The younger children in my ministry were avid Veggie Tales fans. As soon as the 5th grade boys spoke up, however, labeling Veggie Tales "uncool," even the preschoolers who owned Bob the Tomato t-shirts suddenly railed against it. Tailor your lessons and activities towards your 5th and 6th grade boys. The younger children will still be learning even if they do not grasp every single thing, while the older children remain engaged.

Plan short activity segments. Kids have short attention spans regardless of their ages. The older a child gets the longer their attention span is, but short segments work best with today's children. Keep your lesson segments short, so there is less time for disengaged children or disruptions. There are still times when longer segments are needed, especially when responding to the Holy Spirit's leading, but do your best to keep the lesson moving!

Provide extra helpers for your littlest learners. Let's face it, a 4-year-old needs extra help in a lesson designed for upper elementary students. Prepare in advance for extra helpers to be on hand to assist with the younger kids. It's especially helpful when the preschoolers are moving out of the nursery and into the children's ministry. Extra people to remind children that bottoms stay in chairs and extra hands to help with crafts will keep disruptions to a minimum while creating a better learning environment for everyone.

Use concrete language. Abstract and metaphorical language confuses younger children. Cognitively, younger children cannot understand the concept of Jesus living in their heart; they are too literal. Instead of "asking Jesus into your heart," try "become a child of God." Pick the terminology you want to use, making sure it's concrete, and stick to it for all ages, at all times.

Include multiple levels of biblical understanding with each lesson. Obviously, a preschooler is at a much different level biblically and spiritually than a preteen. That does not mean, however, that you need to tailor your lessons to only reach one age group's level of biblical understanding. Each lesson and activities can and should include multiple levels of biblical learning. For example, when teaching about Jesus dying on the cross, explain how Jesus' death was the ultimate atoning sacrifice, while also teaching students that the reason Jesus died was because of His love for us. When multiple levels of biblical learning are being taught, you maximize the number of children being reached.

CREATIVE SOLUTIONS

In addition to the foundations of what multi-aged classrooms should look like, there are a lot of creative things that can be done to make your classroom more effective and enjoyable.

Develop student leaders. A great way to help keep the older children involved is to turn them into leaders. Making them the official paper-passer-outer is not going to keep them engaged. Give the older, more spiritually mature, children a chance to truly lead. Let them discover their gifts and talents through leadership. Do you have children in your ministry who love to sing and dance? Give them the charge of leading the praise and worship music. Can your student leaders be given the task of creating a brand new game for the fall festival? What leadership roles can they have in the classroom? Can they prepare or lead parts of the lesson? Maybe they can read or act out the Bible story during preschool small groups. Develop student leaders out of the older children and watch as God grows them.

Buddy up for reading and writing. Depending on your volunteer pool, you might not have enough adults to assign each non-reader a buddy. What do you do then when lesson activities require reading and writing? Have the children buddy up. This is a great way to involve your older children as leaders, but it's also a great way to foster connectedness and friendship. By making the entire group buddy up, younger less confident readers arc not singled out, and everyone is able to participate in the activity.

Act it out ... without the scripts. Children remember more of what they are taught when they are doing something physical. Acting out the Bible account is a great way to help the lesson stick with them. Many times, however, with the lengthy scripts needing to be read, the younger children cannot participate. Using simple instructions from the leader, serving as the narrator, give the children costumes and props to act out the Bible accounts instead of using scripts. All children, regardless of their reading level, are then able to participate.

Pick games and activities that everyone can play! While a classroom of only older kids is okay when only a handful of children get chosen to play a game, that is often not the case with younger children. Keeping that in mind, remember that it is best to include games that everyone can play. Group games like Four Corners or sit/stand games involve everyone at once and everyone has a chance to be involved.

It's important to also remember the differences between preschoolers and preteens. Preschoolers all want a chance to play, and often get upset if they are not the winner. They also are at a different physical and mental ability than the preteens. Having a 4-year-old race against a 12-year-old isn't fair or very fun for the 4-year-old. While there may be times when you have games tailored for the older children or involving only a handful of children, make sure to include in every lesson games and activities that every child has a chance and the ability to participate in.

Props and visuals will make your lesson come alive. It's not just the younger children who will benefit from props and visuals, the older ones will too. Not only is it involving another one of their senses, helping children to retain that knowledge they just absorbed, but it helps to keep the children engaged. Which sounds more fun to you: hearing about the pieces in the armor of God, or seeing cardboard pieces of armor being put on a volunteer? Younger children need props and visuals to keep them engaged, but everyone benefits from it!

SEE THE BLESSING

Small churches are often set up with a multi-aged children's ministry. Due to its uniqueness and challenges, leaders oftentimes find themselves frustrated or discouraged with their set-up. Don't be discouraged, thinking that because you don't have enough children in your ministry, you're not able to age divide. Think of it as a blessing, that you don't have to age divide.

All I have known in children's ministry is the multi-aged classroom model. Yes, there are challenges and each class dynamic can present its own unique set of challenges. If I had my choice, however, of teaching a classroom full of mixed ages with all the challenges that may occur, or teaching same-aged classes, hands down I would pick the multi-aged classroom, every time. Sometimes you might have to get creative with how you do things in a multi-aged classroom, but it's not impossible. See the blessings, not the challenges. It's worth it.

Amber Pike is a children's minister, writer, wife, and mom of two in LaGrange, KY. She spends her days homeschooling, taking care of her family, and getting as much accomplished during the baby's nap time as possible!

chapter 24

AN UPSIDE-DOWN VIEW OF YOUR COMMUNITY

Do a double-take

BY DANA WILLIAMS

IN 4TH GRADE, MY CLASS took a field trip to the airport for a unit on aviation. As with most school-sponsored field trips, we had a little down time to wait. I vividly remember sitting with my classmates on a commercial plane while our prepared teacher pulled out a book called *Stories with Holes*. She'd read a story to us and we'd devour the challenge to find the loophole that made the puzzling stories make sense. We'd ask questions. We'd throw out off-the-wall ideas. We'd visit and re-visit the details until we made sense of it all. I have a lot of nostalgia for that hot afternoon on a plane with my teacher, my classmates, and a new challenge.

Experiences like this one shaped me and my ability to look at the world in an upside-down way. In ministry, that has served me well, because God's way often seems upside-down to our conventional ways of doing things. As our teacher fed us story after story, our skills at creatively solving the mystery improved. We'd learn new strategies for finding the loopholes that held the keys. Once we learned a strategy, we'd practice it on the next puzzle. We became faster and faster at finding solutions together.

It's a similar experience in ministry. You often face new challenges, new problems, and new pieces that need to fit into the puzzle. Just like a bunch of 4th graders on a hot airplane, you can find creative solutions better and faster as you practice creative strategy. Here are a few strategies to get you looking at your community in an upside-down way that will bring God the glory.

ROOM TO GROW

When I was a little girl, I remember going shoe shopping with my parents. We had a ritual each time I'd try on a new pair of shoes. After they'd remove the packing materials and help me put the shoe onto my foot, we'd tie it. I'd take a few steps around the store and go back to my parents for the inspection. They'd put their thumb on the toe box and try to find my big toe through the shoe. When my toe was discovered in relation to the end of the shoe, they'd say, "Yep, room to grow!" One of the criteria for shoe purchases in our home was that I always had room to grow. My parents were hardworking, but we didn't have the resources to buy new shoes every month, so room to grow was a necessity.

When you're restructuring or changing something in your ministry, be sure to take some time for the room-to-grow check. If your solution works for your situation exactly as it is today, that's good. Will it work if you grow by 10%, 30%, or 100%? Will you be able to add the right resources or people with that growth or will you need to go back to redeveloping a solution? Implementing a strategy that can grow with you might feel a little ill-fitting at first, but the long-term benefits are worth the awkward first days. If the curriculum calls for expensive materials, maybe that works for your budget with one small group, but will it work when two or more need them? Putting two small group leaders in a room with just a handful of kids might seem like overkill, but does it provide your ministry with open space to welcome guests who can connect to a caring adult and other kids?

Virtually every church of every size needs kids' ministry leaders to step into serving roles. Sometimes you get the "yes" and then you give them too large of a group to lead. Your leaders may be able to manage a room full of kids, but will they be satisfied in how they can minister to that number of kids? Recruiting is hard work, but giving leaders growing room helps them be more successful in the work they do. Happy leaders stick around longer! That means less week-to-week recruiting for you. Give your leaders room to grow.

As you prepare lessons for the kids in your ministry, it's important to build in growing room in the lessons themselves. We recently met with a playground designer to develop some ideas for a preschool playscape. He's an expert on playgrounds. In fact, he even told us that from time to time he'll go watch children play on playground equipment. He wants to learn how they use it and how the equipment measures up as kids approach the challenges the playground has to offer. As he shared ideas, certain equipment was off limits to our project because the challenges needed to stretch a preschooler, but not be too difficult or too dangerous. If we'd been designing a playground for elementary students, the off-limits equipment would have flip-flopped in order to provide appropriate challenges. In creating spiritual growth experiences for kids, you need to approach it much like the playground designer and offer appropriate activities and experiences. You want to challenge and stretch their abilities just enough that they have room to grow into the next level without frustrating them by giving them ill-fitting experiences for knowing God better.

The room-to-grow check can be used on everything from seating to rooms and from curriculum to take-home sheets.

Put your thumb on the pieces of your ministry and discover if it's too snug or too large. Look for that sweet spot that gives you a little room to grow into your next level! That next leve may be reaching out into your community in a new way.

INSPECT THE WALLS

God put it in Nehemiah's heart to examine the walls of Jerusalem. They were in disrepair, broken down, and destroyed by fire. The walls should have protected the people of the city, but the walls themselves needed someone to protect and care for them. In Nehemiah 2:11-16, Nehemiah make a decision to go out and take a look around. His mission was to observe and collect information about the state of the walls. He and a few men went out at night to record the broken places and the needs of the city.

Most of our cities today no longer have physical walls for protection. Our neighborhoods and our cities do have places that are in need of protection and care. What would it look like for you to partner with a few trusted people and observe those spaces? Who is hurting? What needs do they have? Are families healthy and thriving? What about the financial situation of your neighborhood? Could education or assistance benefit the community? What challenges do people in your city face?

In some communities, as you assess the needs, it may be overwhelming. I can imagine Nehemiah traveling those walls and sighing as he accounted for crumbled rock and ashes where walls and gates should have been. Pay attention to the challenges your neighborhood faces that break your heart. They may help direct the next steps God has for you.

I think it's interesting to note that the Bible records that Nehemiah went out and did this inspection without any kind of official stamp of approval on it. Maybe that verse gives us a glimpse into the personality of Nehemiah. Based on other pieces of his story, he seems like a rule-following kind of guy to me. So for him, stepping out of his comfort zone of human rules was significant. If you're naturally a within-the-lines kind of person, notice how God nudged Nehemiah to do the task God wanted him to do without a committee. Get out there. Invite someone to lunch. Sit by someone different at the ball game. Listen to their stories. Ask good questions. Ask God to reveal the invisible broken places in your community to you.

THE STRATEGY BELONGS TO GOD

With your fingers on the pulse of your city, ask God to show you the next steps He wants for you to lead for a restoration effort in your community. If you live in an affluent area, it may be a greater challenge to see the needs, much less convince people that God wants to heal them. Wealth can blind people of their spiritual need for God. In those cases, I'm reminded of Paul's declaration to the men of Athens. He stood up among them and spoke of walking through their city and noticing the altars. He points out an altar they dedicated to an unknown god and begins declaring the one true God. The Greeks prided themselves in their knowledge, so he approached them with an explanation that would satisfy their ignorance. Their real need was for God, not for the knowledge, but he employed their love of knowledge to introduce them to God.

When Nehemiah had discovered the exact needs of the walls, he made a decision to restore the walls. He petitioned those in charge for their support of his efforts. He drew from the approval he had from the king to make these changes to convince them. Most of the Jewish leaders were convinced and joined his efforts.

As with any change, there were those who opposed Nehemiah's plan. They mocked and ridiculed them. You will have people who do not agree with the creative plans you make to restore broken places in your community. It's scary to walk outside the walls that make you feel safe and secure, even if they're crumbling down. When the opposition comes,

Nehemiah didn't lean on the approval of the human leaders he had. He went straight to the source. He went to the One who prompted his broken heart for the city and declared that God would give them the success. He aligned himself with the King of the Universe and recognized that it's really not his plan at all. He was a servant of the One who sent him. When the nay-sayers rise up, it's critical for leaders leading strategic change to acknowledge loudly and repeatedly that God owns the strategy. It's not ours. The outcomes aren't ours. We're merely His servants, just like Nehemiah was.

SOMETHING DIFFERENT

Your days are piled high and overflowing with messages. You live in a world where new content is published with the push of a button. I worked in downtown Houston for about three years at one point in my life and I'd often leave the tower I worked in to walk to nearby restaurants for lunch. I'd always see a lot of people out walking. One particular day, I spotted some people walking across a crosswalk and I was compelled to do a double-take because they were dressed in giant bowling pin costumes. A new bowling alley had opened in the area and they wanted to be noticed. It was so unusual that I snapped a photograph and posted it online. It was interesting, but those bowling pins didn't have much effect on my life. I think I bowled there twice. The messages heaped on us can be overwhelming at times and it can sound more like noise than messages that matter.

There's a message that matters. Nothing compares to the message of God's love. When you tell His story well, it stands out among the other noise. His love should make people do a double-take. So, in your creative strategy, consider how you might elevate this incredible message in a way that makes people do a double-take. How can you help your community see that there's something different about God's message of love? Paul used an altar to an unknown god to point to the true message of God's love. The Athenians could relate to the altar and it built a bridge for a conversation about God's love for them. What might that look like in your context? Who knows, it could even be a bowling pin costume that points people to God's incredible love!

PRACTICE CREATIVE STRATEGY

As you approach change and problems with creativity, practice these strategies: Give your ministry just enough room to grow into the next level. Follow Nehemiah's example and take time to observe and assess the needs in your community. Ask God for direction and remember that He owns the strategy to meet those needs. Have fun with creatively cutting through the noise to cause people to do a double-take at God's tremendous love for them.

As the NextGen Pastor at Sugar Grove Church of Christ in Meadows Place, TX, **Dana Williams** is helping parents raise a generation of kids who are for God and for neighbor because of the Gospel. She's fairly confident that she could survive on tacos (if push came to shove), and she's one of the rare ones who loves having her house full of teenagers!

chapter 25

INSPIRATION NOT PERSPIRATION

It's all around you

BY ROB LIVINGSTON

WHEN YOU HEAR THE WORD "creativity," does it make you smile or cringe? When someone asks you if you're creative, do you start sweating nervously or does your mind start spinning with ideas?

How do you find inspiration and where do you find that inspiration that will fuel your creativity. Your inspiration can come from a variety of places. Some find their inspiration for creativity at certain places or locations. Some others find their creativity from other leaders and conferences. In this fast-paced world of social media, you can easily search for your next idea with the touch of a button.

While your number one source of information should be God and the Bible, you can also find inspiration in God's creation.

Some people sit on the beach and watch waves crash while others may go on a hike in the mountains. Others find their inspiration while walking in the early morning and watching the sunrise while others can sit and watch the sunset and envision various areas of their ministry where they need to be a little more creative. Speaker and Author Bob Goff shares in his book *Love Does* his secret location where he finds inspiration. "I do all my best thinking on Tom Sawyer Island at Disneyland. There's a picnic table at the end of a little pier right across from the pirate ship. I suppose most people think this place is just a prop because there are a couple of wooden kegs marked 'gun-powder' and some pirate paraphernalia hung over the railings. But it's not just a prop to me; it's my office."

Finding your inspiration can come from a walk in the woods or the crashing of the waves. It could even come from a "quiet" spot at Disneyland, but sometimes creativity can hit you right in the cereal aisle. Let me explain. A few years ago I was searching for the next theme for our children's worship time. I struggled to come up with what God wanted me to do. I felt like He wanted me to do something with food, but it just wasn't clear until I stopped by my local grocery store one afternoon. I walked down the cereal aisle when all of a sudden I stopped, or should I say God stopped me. I stood for a few minutes just looking at the boxes and then I sat down. There I was ... plopped down in the cereal aisle of this grocery store for about 15 minutes as God revealed the next series and inspired my creativity to write four lessons on popular cereals. Creative inspiration can come from just about anywhere. You just have to be ready to stop and listen. Stop and think about places in your walk of life that can become inspirational spots.

Another source of inspiration can be other leaders in children's ministry, as well as conferences. In the children's ministry world, if you're willing to travel, there's no shortage of conferences. It's at these conferences when the Lord can use various breakout sessions, worship experiences, or main stage speakers to inspire your creativity as you hear how He has worked in others' lives. Conferences give you time to network with other leaders just like you, as well as resource providers and ministry coaches. The people you meet at conferences can help ignite creativity just by sitting and sharing ideas.

Some of these leaders have chimed in on where they find their inspiration.

I find my inspiration driving with Christian music blaring, at restaurants, in toy stores, from Steve Spangler Science videos, and when wandering around home improvement stores taking photos. (You want to get a store employee to come help you? Just whip out a camera and start taking photos of their unusual inventory.) I also love to dwell on a single word and explore all the associations I can make to it. That's when things start happening.

Tina Houser

Children's Pastor, Author,
and Founder of Tina Houser Ministries

I drink coffee and provide space for my mind to explode with ideas. I am an idea factory. I then journal about them, and think on the idea while driving long distances. I share some ideas with close friends to see if there's resonance with that idea.

Josh Denhart

Former Children's Pastor and Owner of
the Amazing Chemistry Show

My creativity is centered in pressure. Necessity is the mother of invention. I find my greatest creativity in problems that need solutions with deadlines. I love a blank page. White space and liberty really accelerate the creative process.

Jeff McCullough

Global Musicianary and founder of Jumpstart3

Inspiration is one of those things that doesn't always show up right when you want it to. For me it's something that I've learned to look for every day ... not just when I need it! When I train my brain to watch for creative ways to connect everyday things in life to God's Word, I find that creative inspiration shows up all over the place! I find it when playing games with my kids. (What if we all played this game by making up our own rules? We NEED to know what the rules really are, don't we?) I find it working on home projects. (God made us to be more like tools than trophies! We aren't saved to be put on a shelf, but to do good works in His name.) I see it in relationships. (I have two sons who came to our family through adoption. We are adopted as sons into God's family!) I see props on stage at high school plays and think, "Hmmm, that would be cool in the kids' wing."

Chuck Peters

Director of Operations at Lifeway Kids

For me the biggest blockage to being creative is having a head so full of things to do that I don't have any space left for new ideas. The solution? Find a way to output your things to do so they get out of your head. I use a phone app where I write down everything that needs to be done, and every morning I check that app to prioritize my list. Doesn't sound very creative, does it? Well it's not. But, when your head isn't so cluttered, it unblocks the channels and the ideas flow!

Mark Millard

The Lads

I gain inspiration from God's Word! We are creative by design. Each of us may jumpstart our creativity in different ways, but for me it starts with knowing how I was made and making time to meditate, think, and ponder on creative outcomes. It's how I approach ministry and life.

Jim Wideman
Former Associate Pastor and President
Jim Wideman Ministries

Literally everywhere. Music. Movies. Fashion. Award Show graphics and performances. I'm inspired by things I read. Great statements in sermons and scriptures. There's a book I love by Twyla Tharp, The Creative Habit. Twyla is a choreographer and says "Make an empty space in any corner of your mind and creativity will instantly fill it." I believe that's true. Create space to let your mind wander and dream. Take those ideas and inspirations and build something on them.

Yancy Wideman Richman
Yancy Ministries

As you can see from these amazing leaders in the kidmin world there are many places to find and grow your creativity. As I read and reread these answers, one idea kept jumping out at me. You must create space in your mind and lives so that your creativity has a place to grow!

I Love Kidmin, Kidmin Spaces and Places, and *Children's Pastors Only* are just a few of the Facebook group pages for kidmin leaders like you. These pages have thousands of children's ministers from across the world just waiting to share or see the next best thing in children's ministry. From stage designs and curriculum to creative ways to recruit volunteers, these Facebook pages have a plethora of ideas to help spark creativity. Not far behind Facebook, you can find many of the leaders in kidmin on Instagram and Twitter. Social media has the ability to inspire new creations and share ideas across the globe. Probably the guru of them all when it comes to creative ideas has to be everyone's favorite, Pinterest. With all of this technology available in the palm of your hand, the ideas are endless. One word of caution, however, when it comes to social media as a source of inspiration. Do not let the ease of social media extinguish your creative flame.

Utilize the tools God has provided for you in your ministry. Surround yourself with others who can challenge you to keep an innovative mindset. However, even with all these various ways you can find inspiration, you must not forget that the first place you should look for inspiration for your creativity is God's Word. *"For we are God's handiwork, created in Christ Jesus to do good works, which God prepared in advance for us to do"* (Ephesians 2:10, NIV).

CPSIA information can be obtained
at www.ICGtesting.com
Printed in the USA
LVHW04s0116220918
590983LV00002B/4/P

9 781943 294787